5
MINUTE
SELLING

ALEX GOLDFAYN

5

MINUTE
SELLING

THE PROVEN, SIMPLE SYSTEM
THAT CAN DOUBLE YOUR SALES...
EVEN WHEN YOU DON'T HAVE TIME

WILEY

Library of Congress Cataloging-in-Publication Data:

ISBN 978-1-119-68765-8 (hardback)
ISBN 978-1-119-68770-2 (ePDF)
ISBN 978-1-119-68768-9 (epub)

Cover design and image: Wiley

Printed in the United States of America

10 9 8 7 6 5 4 3 2 1

To Lisa, who makes our lives possible with quiet elegance and grace.

And to Bella and Noah, who both inspire me daily and teach me that anything is possible.

CONTENTS

A NOTE ABOUT SELLING IN THE POST-PANDEMIC WORLD

I completed writing this book in early 2020, pre-Covid 19, pre-lockdown. It was written in normal times, for normal times.

In the ensuing months, the world changed dramatically, and with it, business.

In turn, the selling process was turned upside down:

Outside salespeople could no longer be on the road.

Nearly *all* salespeople started working remotely, from home.

So did most of our customers.

And so, the rules of engagement have changed.

And you will find that, compared to "normal times," all of the proactive selling techniques described in this book are even more important and effective in a world changed by pandemic.

This is because *5-Minute Selling* is about systematically communicating with our customers and prospects, and showing them that we care about them.

It's about being more present.

It's about helping more customers more.

And our customers *need* this more than ever. Especially in a crisis, or a recession.

They haven't heard from a lot of salespeople during the pandemic lockdown, nor after.

My clients reported nearly unanimously during the lockdown that their competition was *not* calling on their customers. I heard varying versions of this quote countless times: "My customers report that I'm the only one calling them. The competition must not care."

Think about your own phone during the lockdown. Were suppliers calling much? As you'll read in this book, suppliers don't call very much in *good* times.

Now? Most of your competition is in a defensive position.

As I write this, very few salespeople are on offense.

It's understandable. Salespeople are paralyzed by fear. And not just fear of rejection, but fear of job loss; fear for their families; fear for their health.

Here's the thing though: our customers are also afraid. For their health. For their families. For their jobs.

Our customers need us now.

Your customers need you, especially now.

Don't leave them stranded.

Be present.

And guess what?

This is far easier post-pandemic than in normal times.

Your customers are far more available during this crisis, and in its aftermath.

You can reach anybody you want, because nearly everybody is available.

Many of our customers are working at home. Nobody is traveling. Nobody is going to meetings except virtual ones.

It's interesting that post pandemic, with the decrease in in-person selling, the telephone is our single most important tool.

Post-pandemic, the telephone is just as important to successful selling as it was in the 1970s and 1980s, before email.

Luckily, a significant portion of this book is about quickly planning your highest-impact proactive calls, and making them. You'll learn who to call and what to say, and a variety of ways to ask them what you can help them with.

And you'll develop an expertise that will help you succeed now – during this difficult time – and also one that will serve you well for years and decades to come.

So let's play some offense.

Let's go help our customers and prospects.

Let's help them through this time.

And as a result, they will remember you forever.

And they will reward you with business now, and for many years to come.

Good luck, and best wishes for good health and great success.

Alex Goldfayn
May 15, 2020

ACKNOWLEDGMENTS

Today I run a thriving consulting business, but it hasn't always been this way. Multiple times in our lives, my wife of 19 years, Lisa, and I have been flat out of money. Thankfully, those years are distant in the rearview mirror, but the thing I remember most about those times is that in the early years, when we were in our 20s, she believed in me more than I believed in myself. That means, quite literally, that neither this book, nor the four before it, nor, quite frankly, anything else that I've attained professionally would have happened without her support, grace, invaluable input, and love.

My children, 11-year-old twins Bella and Noah, are my reason for doing this work and enduring the risks and travails of entrepreneurship. They're a daily inspiration to me: Noah is deeply insightful, effortlessly analytical, wise beyond his years, and playful, and he has a depth of self-control and determination that most adults would be thrilled to have. Meanwhile, Bella is incredibly focused and strong, has a wicked sense of humor, and is a wonderful friend to those who are close to her. She's also a world-class expert at perseverance, particularly when it comes to her chosen sport of ninja, at which she excels. I work to make these amazing little people proud.

My parents, Leon and Jane Goldfayn, brought me to America from the former Soviet Union when I was two years old, with a tiny bit of cash and two suitcases. They showed courage and strength that I'm not sure I could summon even today, with all of the resources I have at my disposal. They've been a singular example of hard work and perseverance throughout my life. Without them pulling the family out of there, I'd be living in a Soviet-era apartment, and this book would be in Russian.

My 94-year-old grandmother Bella continues to teach me positivity, joy, and belief in the good things to come. She has always been as grateful as I am to be here in America. We share that bond.

Our family—Ron and Jan Lobodzinski, Keith Lobodzinski, along with Greg, Jeannie, and Sean Livelsberger—are an island of calm support in the storm of life. The Goldfayns know you are always there for us, and it's mutual.

Solo consulting can be a lonely business for some, but I feel none of that because I am lucky to enjoy friendships with my clients. I am grateful for the partnership of Don Maloney, A.J. Maloney, Christy Maloney, Patrick Maloney, Michael Maloney, Paul Lee, Gary Bernstein, Rich Collins, Paul Van Duyne, Jeff Pratt, Ted Lerman, Carl Parker, Jeff New, Jordan New, Dan New, Joe Velleman, Ben Hannewyk, Charlton Keultjes, Charles Ciccarello, James Roth, Bob Luckenbaugh, Renee Roth, Bob Brister, Nick Brister, Pete Traeger, Doug O'Rourke, Michael Whiteside, Scott Barbour, Mike Adelizzi, Matt Sanderson, and Chris Mundschenk. I am happy to drink with all of you!

My executive admin, Jenna Jessup, handles myriad small details so that I can focus on the big ones. Her strengths help me implement mine. I've said for nearly 20 years that I won't have employees, but I'm sure glad I have Jenna!

My fellow solo consultant colleague and good friend Wes Trochlil is always happy to share his thinking, whether I ask for it or not. Most times, I'm quite happy to receive his opinion, and when I'm not, he tells me anyway! He's an excellent sounding board, and he has helped me countless times over the years.

I'm also thankful for my long-term friendships with Chris Patterson and Jeff Conroy. They have imparted much invaluable wisdom over the years without which my business would not be where it is today.

My wife and I are lucky to have wonderful friends. We are particularly appreciative of our bond with Amir and Sakeena Haq, and Ben and Kendall Haight. You are family to us, and we are grateful to have you close to us, literally and figuratively.

Finally, thank you to my friend and distinguished editor Richard Narramore and his crew at John Wiley & Sons. This is our third consecutive book together. My previous book with him, *Selling Boldly*, became a *Wall Street Journal* bestseller, and the idea for this book came about over several phone calls. We thought of it together. If Richard thinks it's a good idea, I know it will work. That's a big deal! I also appreciate the hard work of the high-level Wiley professionals Peter Knox, Victoria Anllo, and Elisha Benjamin. Tiffany Taylor copy-edited the manuscript with a light but detailed touch. Thank you all.

ABOUT THE AUTHOR

Alex Goldfayn grows companies.

He is the CEO of The Revenue Growth Consultancy, which works with organizations to install positive mindsets and systems of simple behaviors that routinely generate an additional 10–20% in new sales annually.

His clients include manufacturers, distributors, and business-to-business service organizations—typically in mature industries—that make the world go around. Revenue growth projects with Alex typically run for 6 to 12 months and include multiple in-person and remote learning experiences for customer-facing teams, as well as detailed tracking, scorekeeping, accountability, and recognition components.

Not only does Alex regularly implement the systems in this book for his clients, but he also applies the approaches in his own firm, one of the highest-grossing and most successful solo consulting practices of any kind in America.

Throughout the year, Alex delivers more than 75 workshops and keynote speeches for companies, executive groups, and associations.

His previous book is the *Wall Street Journal* bestseller *Selling Boldly*. He is also the author of *The Revenue Growth Habit* (which 800-CEO-Read selected as its sales book of the year) and *Evangelist Marketing*.

Alex lives with his wife and 11-year-old twins in the Chicago area.

If you'd like to discuss applying the systems in this book with Alex, please call him directly at 847-459-6322 or email alex@goldfayn.com.

DOWNLOAD YOUR PLANNERS AND TRACKERS

The planners, trackers, and actions checklist that appear here in *5-Minute Selling* are available as a free download on my web site, www.Goldfayn.com. Various tools and programs to help you with action and accountability are also available.

Go there, download them, and *use them* to grow your sales.

5-Minute Selling is a *system* for making more money by proactively communicating with customers and prospects.

PREFACE:
THIS BOOK IS A SYSTEM

An action is something you do once. It is fleeting.

But a *system* is made up of actions that you do consistently and repeatedly over time.

One-off actions are snowflakes, melting on the pavement. They only exist for a moment, and then they are gone. But systems create blizzards.

This book is a system. It will create a blizzard of more sales, larger orders, and more customers.

Knowing what's in this book won't make you any money. (And you already know most of what you will read.) But *doing it* will change your life.

And in *5-Minute Selling*, it is my singular purpose to help and motivate you to do the work. I am trying to push and plead and ask and convince you to take the 16 lightning-fast and simple actions laid out in Part 4 of this book.

In five minutes of easy daily effort, I will show you how to significantly and predictably increase your sales as my clients do. As more than 10,000 of my salespeople clients and live workshop attendees have done over the years.

Many have added 10, 20, or 50% to their sales. Some have doubled their sales. Their stories are at the end of nearly every chapter of this book.

The steps I lay out here are proven. The system is simple. It's a system for making more money by helping more customers more.

It works. We know it works.

It's not new. It has been around for years. It's not merely theory in a book. It is applied by thousands of sales professionals daily.

I lay out *exactly* what my clients do to dramatically grow their sales in five minutes a day. It's all here in this short, fast book. (If the system takes five minutes per day, the book can't take weeks to read!)

Can you give me five minutes a day to sell a lot more and bring home more money to your family? Because we don't need more than five. Give me five minutes daily, and I'll give you a system for helping your customers more and improving your family's life.

5
MINUTE
SELLING

PART ONE

INTRODUCING THE 5-MINUTE SELLING SYSTEM

CHAPTER 1

WHAT IS THE 5-MINUTE SELLING SYSTEM?

The 5-Minute Selling System consists of two planners to help you lay out your proactive calls and follow-ups for the coming week, and two trackers where you can record your progress and success.

The 5-Minute Selling System consists of implementing *any* of the 16 proactive communications actions listed in this chapter and Part 4 of this book for a combined total of five minutes per day and writing down the results on the Action Tracker in this chapter.

We will use two planning tools and two tracking tools. I will introduce them in this chapter and then revisit them throughout the book where it makes sense.

The approach is to *communicate* with customers and prospects proactively for a combined 5 minutes per day, or 25 total minutes weekly.

You'll need to spend five to 10 additional minutes intentionally planning your week on Sunday or Monday morning. And you may need another 10 minutes weekly to write down your actions and results to track your success and additional opportunities for following up.

So if you stick to these timelines, we're looking at 55 minutes in a week. Less than an hour to do work that will dramatically increase your sales. It might shoot your sales up 50% or 100%. Is it worth less than one hour out of a 40-hour week to focus on increasing your sales that much?

Can you do more than five minutes a day? Of course. You're welcome to.

The more you communicate with customers and prospects, the more they buy. And the less you communicate, the less they buy.

More on these five daily minutes at the end of this chapter.

The Proactive Communications

Here are the 16 actions that make up the 5-Minute Selling System:

THE 5-MINUTE SELLING SYSTEM

Do any combination of these proactive communications with customers and prospects for five total minutes every day. Record your progress in the 5-Minute Action Tracker.

Proactive Phone Calls	Proactive Communications
✓ Call Your Current Best Customers (PC-BestC)	✓ Offer Additional Products and Services to Existing Customers (DYK)
✓ Call Small & Medium Customers to Make Them Bigger (PC-SmallC)	✓ Ask What Else Your Customers Need or Buy Elsewhere (rDYK)
✓ Call Customers You Haven't Talked to in Three Months or More (PC-3moC)	✓ Follow Up on Pre-Quote Opportunities (PreQFU)
✓ Call Customers Who Used to Buy But Stopped (PC-GoneC)	✓ Follow Up on Quotes & Proposals (QFU)
✓ Call Customers Who Recently Received an Order or Service (PC-PD)	✓ Review Order History & Ask About Products Previously Purchased (OH)
	✓ Ask for the Business (Pivot)
✓ Call Prospects You're Engaged In Active Buying Conversations With (PCPro-BC)	✓ Ask Happy Customers for a Referral (Refer)
	✓ Ask Your Customers What Percent of Their Business You Have, and Then Ask for More (%Biz)
✓ Call Prospects You Know Are Buying Elsewhere (PCPro-Else)	✓ Send Handwritten Notes (Note)
✓ Call Prospects You've Never Talked to (PCPro-1C)	✓ Email DYK Weekly (eDYK)

As you can see, the entire left side consists of proactive phone calls, which are a big focus for this work. There are eight different kinds of people you can call: five are customers, and three are prospects.

These calls will often result in a voicemail, and I will teach you how to leave a really effective one (see Chapter 15).

On the right side are 10 proactive communications that do not require you to dial out. They can be made on your existing calls, with customers who call in throughout the day. You certainly *can* call customers to make these communications, but you don't need to. Many of these communications— including the fast-acting *did you know* question (DYK— Chapter 25) and *reverse did you know* question (rDYK— Chapter 26) are single questions, requiring 3 seconds to ask and another 10 seconds to write down.

There is a brief chapter on each of the 16 actions on this list in Part 4 of this book.

QUICKLY PLANNING YOUR UPCOMING WEEK OF PROACTIVE OUTREACH

Because making proactive communications is not the default position for most of us salespeople, we need to be intentional about this work so that it can become a habit.

We need to write down *who* we will reach out to and follow up with. This helps us think about people we wouldn't usually talk to during the week and, more importantly, *keeps them in front of our eyes during the week so that we remember to call them.* To this end, I am arming you with two quick planners.

Here is the Proactive Call Planner:

5 MINUTE SELLING — PROACTIVE CALL PLANNER	
My Best Customers Who Can Buy More	**Customers Who Used to Buy but Stopped**
My Smaller and Medium Customers Who Can Buy More from Me	**Customers Who Recently Received Products or Services — Follow Up**
Customers I Haven't Talked to in 3 Months or More	**PROSPECTS I Am Having Active Buying Conversations With — Follow Up**
PROSPECTS I Once Talked to, but They Did Not Buy — Follow Up	**PROSPECTS I Know Are Buying Elsewhere**

Download all the 5-Minute Selling Planners and Trackers at www.goldfayn.com | Copyright 2020 Alex Goldfayn

This is where to quickly think through who you will call this week. Three minutes of writing here is enough to load you up with five business days' worth of calls. Not 30 minutes, but 3 minutes.

Another quick tool for you to spend a few minutes with at the beginning of your week is the Weekly Follow-Up Planner:

WEEKLY
FOLLOW-UP PLANNER

Week of (Date):

Customers with Pre-Quote or Pre-Proposal Opportunities to Follow Up With	Customers With Quotes or Proposals to Follow Up With	Current Customers Who Can Buy More Who I Can Follow Up With (And What to Offer Them)

This is a place to write down the three most important, lowest-hanging kinds of opportunities to follow up on in the coming week.

I recommend that you use these two planners for no more than three minutes each at the beginning of the week. Write down as many names as you can in the three minutes. More guidance on how to use each planner is in Chapter 11. This chapter is a quick overview. Later, we'll dive deeper.

QUICKLY TRACKING

Planning lets us organize our thoughts and quickly prepare ourselves for proactive actions during the week. Then, throughout the week, mostly in quick bursts that take seconds, not minutes, we do the work.

As the work gets done, I'd like you to quickly write it down. If you don't want to *write*, you can *type*.

It doesn't matter how you plan and track—it only matters that you quickly plan and quickly track. This way, you can track your successes.

You know what's working. *And most importantly, you know what to follow up on.*

First, consider using a quote tracker.

Most organizations do not have a *complete and accurate* list of quotes that have gone out. This Quote Tracker is a simple tool, but it can be revolutionary to your sales success. As in, it can double your sales *on its own,* just by you knowing what quotes are out there that you need to follow up on. Many more details on this Quote Tracker are in Chapter 12.

QUOTE TRACKER

Week of (Date):

Quote Date	Quote #	Customer / Prospect Name	Products / Services	Amount $	Follow-Up 1		Follow-Up 2		Follow-Up 3	
					How	When	How	When	How	When

And here is the Action Tracker you can use to write down your proactive actions, progress, and results throughout the week:

5-MINUTE SELLING ACTION TRACKER

Week of (Date):

Day / Date	Customer / Prospect Name	Proactive Action Code	What You Said	What They Said	$$ E, EA, Q/P, C

Total Opened Business: **Total Opened Annualized:**   **Total Quoted / Proposed:**   **Total Closed:**

This is a place to log each action and write a quick note about what you said, and what the customer or prospect said. The last column is where you'll note the dollar value of your efforts—even if the opportunity has merely been opened or progressed. I want you to connect dollar values to your three-second proactive actions.

Each action should take a maximum of 20 seconds to write down. Not 20 minutes, but 20 seconds. Read more about this tracker in Chapter 13.

Remember, you can download these tools on my web site at www.Goldfayn.com.

THE SYSTEM IS THE KEY TO YOUR SALES GROWTH

This is the thing that my thousands of successful client sales-people most attribute their success to: *the system.*

These pieces of paper will prepare you for success each week and *prove* your success to you. They will hold you accountable, because you need to write things down.

They will *remind* you to make some high-speed proactive communications daily. They will remove self-doubt and make you bold, because your tracker pages will be filled with successes and wins.

And in this work, the wins come very quickly.

Offer a customer an additional product, and, statistically, one out of five such offers will be accepted and purchased. Follow up on a quote or proposal, and, statistically, we know that one out of five follow-ups will close.

Call a customer you haven't talked to in three months or more, and have a lovely relationship-building conversation and discuss new opportunities. You'll feel good.

You'll do well.

And your bank account will grow.

BUT IS FIVE MINUTES PER DAY REALLY ENOUGH?

Yes, five minutes of implementing these proactive actions daily is enough.

Some days, you'll spend far less. Some days you'll spend less than a minute, and in that time you'll ask five questions about additional products and services. I call these *did you know* questions, as in, "Did you know we can also help you with this product or that product?" On these one-minute days, you will also have time to ask five *reverse did you know* questions, where you ask the customer about other products they buy elsewhere that you can help them with.

Most of your proactive calls will be done in five minutes or less, and a number of the actions on the right side of the checklist sheet can be done during these calls.

Will some calls go longer than five minutes? They can, but they don't have to. You can easily accomplish everything you need in these calls in less than five minutes.

Want do more than five minutes? You should feel free, if the spirit moves you.

This is fun, positive work because you are helping the customer while helping yourself, your company, and your family. In the 5-Minute Selling System, you offer more value to your customers and prospects, and they reward your effort by buying it!

You help them more, and they pay you for it. That's a pretty good way to live.

That's 5-Minute Selling.

5-MINUTE SELLING SUCCESS

Every chapter from this one to Chapter 34 will end with a real success story from a salesperson or other customer-facing professional. My goal with these is two-fold: first, I hope to motivate and energize you to implement the 5-Minute Selling System; and second, I want to prove to you that this stuff works, and quickly.

These are all people who have participated in a revenue-growth project with me wherein we grow my client's (their employer's) firm between 10—20% on average. I've made a few necessary edits to these stories: I've made them anonymous for a variety of mostly obvious reasons, and I've changed the names. But all the details are real, as are the people who experienced them.

Here is the first one.

"I've had a phenomenal year applying your sales growth habits. I think the best thing about them is that you stay focused on doing something every day, every week, every month, to keep stuff moving through the sales funnel. It infuses a discipline into my sales work. So even when one is busy with projects, billing payroll, technical problems, or whatever, one can ALWAYS make time to move the sales process forward just a bit." —Mike D., project manager at a service company.

CHAPTER

2

I Don't Want You to Read This Book, I Want You to Do This Book

This work can double your sales in lightning-fast, multi-second bursts throughout the day.

I don't want you to read this book. I want you to *do* this book.

That's because reading leads to knowing, but knowing doesn't make us any money. Knowing won't make you a dollar.

Not only that, but as I say in every speech and workshop: *you already know everything you're about to read.* There's nothing new here. You know this.

But *doing* is different than knowing.

It's the doing that helps our customers more. It's the doing that helps us bring home more money for our family. It's the doing that helps us hit our number and then fly past it.

Knowing is for professors—let *them* know.

But doing is for *us.* Sellers *do.* And *5-Minute Selling* is all about the doing.

WHY I WROTE THIS BOOK

If you follow my work, you might be wondering how this book is different than my other books.

In 2011, I wrote *Evangelist Marketing,* which is all about the company-to-many track of communications. It's mostly about list-based marketing.

In 2015, *The Revenue Growth Habit* focused on corporate—not individual—sales growth. That is, it lays out systems for business owners and sales executives to implement an early (less evolved) version of this work *with their teams.*

In 2018, *Selling Boldly* dove deeply into the theories and teachings of positive psychology—optimism, confidence, gratitude, and boldness—that are critical to selling more. Like this book, *Selling Boldly* is for individual salespeople, but it's a book primarily about the sales mindset.

Which brings me to *5-Minute Selling.* It's for salespeople and executives who sell—and it's entirely about action. It's all about those five minutes of combined daily action—made up mostly of three-second efforts—that can double or even triple your sales.

It's all about the proactive action.

It's all about the communications with customers and prospects.

It's all about helping you create your *system for growth.*

When you do this book (as opposed to read this book), you will have your weekly and daily processes for sales growth laid out. And then, you will implement them.

I wrote this book to help you understand how lightning-fast and easy it is to grow your sales by a lot. I wrote it to help you understand exactly what to do to make it so. And I wrote it to help you go do these things.

What's the Best Time to Implement Your 5-Minute Selling Techniques?

Early morning. First thing, if possible.

Before the phone calls, problems, and complaints start coming in. Before your colleagues begin coming to you with questions and issues. Before you're fatigued from the day's hoop-jumping—and there *will* be hoops.

These proactive actions are inherently uncomfortable. They require us to overcome some fear of rejection.

As such, we'll need to lean on our confidence and optimism to implement this work, especially when first starting. And for most people, these two mindsets are at their highest levels first thing in the morning, before complaining customers start to wear us down.

The experts tell us that all challenging things should be done first thing in the morning. Want to exercise? Do it early, before the day gets away from you. Trying to write a book? Write 500 words a day in 30 minutes at 7:00 a.m. (after you exercise).

On a Silver Platter, Here Is How to Make More Money

As with most of these ideas, I am not the originator of this concept. I merely cobble them together into a system and then facilitate my clients' implementation of them.

Now, I am urging you to implement them. I am begging you.

Here are the tools.

Here are the techniques.

Here is the accountability.

Here is the system.

Your family and your customers and your company all deserve for you to do this work. Give them five minutes of proactive-simple-but-maybe-slightly-uncomfortable work each day.

Don't hurt them.

Do these seconds-long communication efforts like *did you know* questions (DYKs), *reverse did you know* questions (rDYKs), and quote follow-ups (QFUs).

Do these quick, proactive calls at a rate of one a day. Do them early. Do them before the day gets away from you.

And enjoy your fast and significant sales growth!

HOW MANY CALLS SHOULD YOU DO?

One or two calls daily is the right number.

Do 1 a day, and you'll make more than 250 phone calls. Two a day gets you to 500 calls. That's enough for dramatic sales growth.

If you want to do more, I encourage it. But you certainly don't need to.

I'M ASKING YOU TO GIVE IT TWO WEEKS

Because of the fast successes, I'm asking you to try 5-Minute Selling for two weeks.

That's 5 minutes a day for 10 days. That's not even 1 hour out of 80 working hours. I'm asking for 1% of your next 80 hours.

Give me 50 minutes over the next 2 weeks to start revolutionizing your sales results. I'll detail more about this in the next chapter.

Now, Let's Go Sell More, in Five Minutes a Day

Now you know what *5-Minute Selling* is all about.

You know sales growth is about implementing a system of proactive communications that you make to customers and prospects in three-second bursts throughout your day. You know it works, and you know the results will come quickly.

I'll show you exactly what to do and how to do it, and arm you with the precise language so you know exactly what to say.

Then you'll do the work. And we'll enjoy your dramatic sales growth together!

5-Minute Selling Success

"Having a selling process like this is really helpful. Now, I know exactly what I need to do every day. Before, my bosses would just say, 'Go sell something.' Now I know who I need to call, and what I need to say to them—and even what products to offer them. It's awesome!" —Rick A., outside salesperson at a distributor in a mature industry.

CHAPTER

3

TAKE THE 5-MINUTE SELLING TWO-WEEK CHALLENGE

Follow the plan in this chapter for two weeks, and you'll see new opportunities and new sales. If your sales cycle is longer than two weeks, you'll make significant progress toward new sales as a result of the following up you will do.

Because the wins in this work come quickly, I have created a simple, guided two-week process for you to begin your sales-growth journey. This is how many thousands of my salespeople clients have dramatically grown their sales in minutes per day. I am showing you what they do.

That's 5 minutes a day for 2 weeks—which is 50 total minutes across 10 business days—and you will see clear, decisive improvements and successes in your sales work.

You will open up additional opportunities.

You will write more quotes and proposals.

You will progress more customers toward a new sale.

You will add new line items to current customers.

Your pipeline will start to expand. And, you will see the beginning of real, predictable sales growth.

You Do Not Need to Read This Entire Book Before Starting the Two-Week Challenge

Don't wait until you've read the book.

Don't read and *then* do. Rather, read *and* do.

Remember, knowing makes no money. Doing makes the money. Get to the doing ASAP.

Here Is Your Two-Week Challenge

Go to my website, Goldfayn.com, click the cover of this book on the home page, and download all of the planning and tracking tools for free.

Now spend a total of five minutes filling out *both* the Proactive Call Planner and the Follow-Up Planner.

That's five minutes total, not five minutes each. Quickly plan and quickly do, okay?

Write names of people in them, not names of companies (although it's okay to include the company if you'd like). We call people, not companies. We build relationships with people, not companies.

Once your planners are filled out, you can move on to making the communications. I list them for Week 1 and Week 2 next.

Week 1 Actions

Here are your minimums for your first week. These are totals for the week, which means I'm asking you for one of each action per day.

5 DYKs: That's one per day, but you can do all five in a single conversation. It takes three seconds to ask a *did you know* question.

5 rDYKs: That's one per day. It takes three seconds to ask a *reverse did you know* question.

5 quote or proposal follow-ups: That's one per day. As you'll see in Chapter 28, email is okay for quote follow-ups. This is a 20-second effort.

5 proactive calls: This is one call per day. You pick who you'd like to call, but make at least one of them a good, warm prospect. Make your call early in the morning. First thing, if possible. You will probably leave a message (one minute, maximum), but if they pick up, you'll have a friendly conversation for a few minutes. Go through the short scripts in Chapters 19–24 for what to say on these calls. If you follow them, these calls should take less than five minutes. Of course, you can decide to go longer if it's going well.

WEEK 2 ACTIONS

We're going to repeat the recipe from Week 1, because I want you to apply what you learn in the first week's work to the second week:

- **5 DYKs**
- **5 rDYKs**
- **5 quote or proposal follow-ups**
- **5 proactive calls** to any kind of customer or prospect you'd like, but make at least *one* of these calls to a warm prospect

That's it.

Four proactive actions per day. Twenty in a week. Forty proactive actions over the two-week challenge.

If you do them, I'd bet my children's college money (which is very important to me) that you'll make new sales, open up new opportunities, and progress existing opportunities toward a close.

THE ACTION COUNTS ARE MINIMUMS

I want to be clear: the four actions per day that I listed are minimums. If you want to do more, you'll sell more.

And since we're talking about three seconds per DYK and rDYK question, it's incredibly easy to double and triple the numbers I'm suggesting here. Remember, one of five DYKs sells over time. If you ask for five in a week, you'll close one each week. But if you ask for five in a day, you'll close one per day! That's a lot more interest.

But it's up to you.

If you do "only" the actions I'm suggesting here, you *will* see results. And my goal is that these results are *so* easy for you to attain that it would be a no-brainer decision for you to continue implementing your 5-Minute Selling System.

REPORT IN AND TELL ME HOW IT'S GOING

Write to me at alex@goldfayn.com—or on LinkedIn or Facebook—and let me know how your two-week challenge is going. I'll reply to every email that comes in! I can't wait to hear all about your successes!

5-MINUTE SELLING SUCCESS

"I've been a *did you know* machine. I just fire rafts of *did you know* questions at my customers, and you know what? I'm constantly surprised about how many products they *don't* know about! I thought everybody knew! I ask *did you know* questions, and they almost always open up conversations about new orders for new products. Just the other day I asked a DYK, and the customer bought it, and if he buys everything he needs of this product for us, it will be worth $100,000 per year."
—Joe F., outside sales at a Canada-based manufacturer.

PART TWO

FOUNDATIONAL PRINCIPLES

CHAPTER

4

90% OF SALESPEOPLE SELL REACTIVELY

Almost all experienced salespeople sell reactively. This is harmful to the customer—and, worse, it's damaging to you and your family.

Most of us salespeople work in a reactive vicious circle that looks like this:

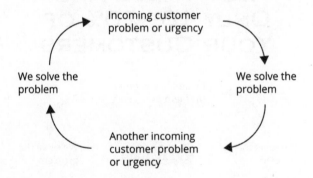

We get in to the office, and almost immediately, a customer calls or writes.

This customer needs something. It's almost always urgent. It's probably a problem.

Something is wrong. Right? And *you* have to fix it.

"Here's a hoop, now jump!"

And you jump. You have to. There is no choice.

This is customer service work, and you have to serve the customer. You cannot say, "I'm sorry, I can't help you right now because I'm doing my proactive communications."

The work is to make the customer happy, and *you are world-class at this*. There are few better. It's what you do. It's what they *expect* you to do. So, you do it.

Once you take care of the problem or urgency with that first customer of the day, what happens? The phone rings again.

Who is on the other end of the line? Another customer, another problem, another hoop to jump through.

"Here's another hoop!"

And like circus seals, we jump. All. Day. Long.

We react to the incoming issues of the day. Then we go home.

The next day, we do it again. And again. And this is how we live—jumping through one hoop after another.

BUT THESE ARE ONLY 10—20% OF YOUR CUSTOMERS

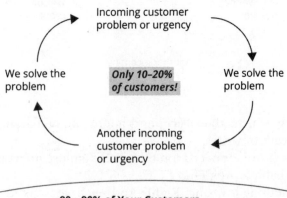

Here's the thing. These customers who are constantly calling and sucking you into the vicious reactive circle? They're only 10–20% of *all* your customers.

They're the ones who complain the most. They're the ones who aren't happy unless they're unhappy. They're the squeaky wheels, right?

The other 80–90% of your customers? They're good! They're happy! *They're not calling, because they're happy.*

They're calling *other* suppliers, though, believe me. They're just not calling *you.*

And here's the tragedy of it all: we're not calling them, either. Because we're so busy with the 10–20% of the customers who are calling us.

And so, these good, quiet customers simply do not hear from us. They don't call us, and we don't call them. There is silence, and they order from us on autopilot.

WHY DOES THIS HAPPEN?

In my estimation, 90% of experienced salespeople are totally reactive to incoming urgencies and problems. Why?

Because you have lots of happy customers. Because you are successful. Because your customers depend on you for your excellent service.

You know who's *not* reactive?

Brand-new salespeople. The ones without any customers.

They have no choice but to be proactive. They need leads, prospects, and activity in general. They make lots of outbound phone calls.

THE TERRIBLE THINGS THAT HAPPEN WHEN WE SELL REACTIVELY

The customers niche us. They know what they buy from us, and they know what they buy elsewhere, *even if we could sell it to them.* It would be easier for them to buy it from us, and we would like to sell it to them, but it's not possible because it's simply not discussed. It doesn't come up. The only things that come up are the issues the customer calls us about. Right now, as you read this, your customers are buying things from the competition that they could be buying from you.

We niche our customers. We know what the customer buys from us, and that's all they buy. We don't discuss other products or services they need. We don't bring up products—in this category or another—that could help them. Why? Because we're too busy reacting. We're too busy jumping through hoops.

All of our customers are affected by our reactivity, not just the ones calling. This affects every customer, even the happy, quiet ones. Because we spend all of our time with the complaining customers (because that's who calls, right?), we don't get to communicate *at all* with the vast majority of our customers who are happy. The ones who deserve our attention. The ones who are our best customers because they buy reliably without demanding a ton of our time. The ones who would be thrilled to buy more from us. They get the short end of the stick—they get less of us—because they are not calling with their problems. It's not fair, is it?

We don't bring up or ask about additional products or services that can help our customers. Who has the time? Your customers bring you fires all day. You have to put them out.

We almost never call out proactively. Again, who has the time? Think about it: how many phone calls do you make to customers and prospects when nothing is wrong, to catch up, build your relationship, and discuss what they're working on these days that you can help with? The fact is, the proactive call has gone nearly extinct. Much of this book is about this proactive phone call. Parts 2 and 3 dive deeply into this old-school tool that will revolutionize your sales results and help your customer a great deal.

We don't follow up on quotes and proposals as much as we should. We're too busy solving problems. We're too busy figuring out how to fit our bodies through the hoops that are in front of us. This is hugely harmful because we've already done nearly all the work to get new sales, but we feel that we don't have the time to reach out and follow up on our quotes and proposals. We feel that we don't have the time to tell our customers that *we* want to help them.

THE BUSINESS IMPACT OF OUR SALES REACTIVITY

When we are totally reactive like this, our success is completely outside of our control.

If the problems we are forced to solve all day lead to additional sales, then we will sell some more. But if these incoming inquiries do *not* lead to additional sales, then so it goes.

We float with the tide. We have no motor, or sail, or rudder. We go where we are taken.

Our success is not up to us. Rather, *it's up to the small percentage of unhappy customers who call us all day long.*

This is a very difficult and terrible way to live. It costs us real money. It costs our family.

And it forces our happy customers to go elsewhere because they don't hear from us. They are forced to buy from lesser providers, who they don't like as much, *because they simply don't know that they can buy from us.*

Selling reactively is basically tragic. This book is the antidote.

Five minutes of intentional, proactive selling executed during your reactive day—much of which can be done on the incoming phone calls you field all day—is the antidote.

5-MINUTE SELLING SUCCESS

"After the workshop we did, I started talking to my customers and finding out about how much they buy from other distributors. I started telling them that *I can sell them those things.* And you know what? They're starting to buy from me now! And we're both better off for it. I'm better than the other guys." —Jennifer A., sales manager at a commodity product distributor.

CHAPTER

5

THE TERRIBLE IMPACT OF REACTIVE SELLING

Reactive selling makes us fearful, meek, pessimistic, and cynical. These mindsets murder sales growth.

Not only does reactive selling cost us real money each year, but it also takes a significant toll on our emotional health.

Because the vast majority of our interactions with customers are negative—they are unhappy about something when they call; nobody calls to ask if they can pay us more money—it makes *us* more negative.

Spending our days dealing with negativity makes us **fearful** of rejection and of losing the customer. It makes us **meek** and **gun-shy**. We believe our customers aren't happy with us, which is simply untrue. But because *we* believe that, we hesitate to call our happy customers and offer them additional value.

Reactive selling makes us **pessimistic**. We expect negativity. We expect problems. We expect unhappy customers. We expect phone calls to go badly. When the phone rings, we automatically think to ourselves, "Oh great, here we go again!"

It makes us **cynical**, which in sales is the opposite of being grateful. This makes us **distrustful**. It makes us believe that our customers don't mean well and are out to get us. It makes us behave accordingly, which is pretty much to run away from these terrible people. Of course, they are not, and we should not, but this is what years of reactive problem-solving leads to.

Finally, reactivity leads to **quick surrenders** and a lack of the perseverance that successful sales requires. We don't keep trying, because we don't believe we will get the business if we try again. Worse, we don't believe that the customers want and need and deserve our help. Instead, we believe the opposite: things always go wrong (it's what we deal with all day, right?).

Now look back at **words in bold** in this chapter. Are these mindsets and traits conducive to sales growth or any kind of success in general? Are they conducive to *happiness?*

The answer is, of course, no. They are conducive to running in place, treading water, or, worse, slowly sinking.

THIS IS HOW *ALL* OF THE COMPETITION THINKS

Here's a really important point for you to take away: this is how the competition operates.

Remember, nearly all salespeople work reactively like this. Including, and *especially,* the competition.

You are actively moving away from these positions. But your competitors are entrenched in them.

The mindsets I identify here occur without salespeople knowing it. It occurs in milliseconds. Your competition suffers from this kind of fearful, negative thinking *without even knowing it.*

You are growing. *You* are starting intentional, proactive outreach to customers and prospects.

They are in a turtle crouch, worrying about what terrible thing will happen next.

Let them. Let them react all day. Let them be terrified and pessimistic and silent.

With the thinking and behaviors you're embarking on here, you're in a position to dominate the competition.

Know this. And behave accordingly.

Boldly!

5-MINUTE
SELLING SUCCESS

"These proactive calls have been great for me. I was uncomfortable with them at first, but you know what? Not one customer has gotten mad at me for calling them. They say that they're happy I called. We talk about what they have coming up, and more times than not, they give me an order. The last one, earlier today, was $18,000 with somebody who hadn't bought from me in over a year." —John C., inside sales, wholesale distributor.

CHAPTER

6

How to Break Out of the Reactive Selling Vicious Circle

The telephone will bust you out of the reactive selling vicious circle. Proactive calls will change your life and quickly impact your sales.

We've established that
reactive selling is harmful to the soul and bank account. We've
established that it hurts customers and us and our families.
And we've laid out that this is how nearly every experienced
salesperson operates, as a simple result of the unrelenting
incoming waves of customer problems and urgencies we're
required to respond to.

So what's the solution? How do we extract ourselves from
this vicious reactive circle?

The key lies in making contact with the 80–90% of your
customers who are not calling with problems and concerns.
The rate-determining step is to talk to customers who are happy.

TESTIMONIAL CALLS

I've written at length in multiple books and countless arti-
cles, videos, and audio podcasts about how to conduct testimonial calls with your happy customers, so we're going to
dive into that here. These calls—about what you're doing
right for them ("so that I can double down on those things
for you")—are the opposite of the problems and urgencies
you discuss with your customers throughout the day.

In the testimonial calls—which are a part of every single project that I do with clients—we ask customers these two simple questions:

- **What are some of your favorite things about working with us?**
- **How does that help you?**

These questions ask the customer to identify positives instead of negatives; value instead of frustrations. And remember, these are the happy customers. *They're not upset about anything!* So they *will* tell you what they think.

Your job is to listen. Hear what they are telling you. *Believe* what they are telling you. Buy what they are saying as the truth.

And then behave accordingly. Which means *behaving confidently and boldly.*

I am being brief here about testimonial calls on purpose, because my last two books, *Selling Boldly* and *The Revenue Growth Habit,* dive deeply into the process and scripting for a successful testimonial call. This book is about a system of action, so that's what we are focusing on here.

PROACTIVE SALES CALLS

If you are so moved, make testimonial calls. You'll have great, uplifting conversations that will fill you with the positive energy and mindset to do this work.

But my thinking on this has developed somewhat, especially for individual salespeople trying to sell more (as opposed to organizational sales growth, which is the crux of my work with clients).

In the last several years, I've seen countless clients bust out of the reactive selling vicious circle *simply by making proactive phone calls to customers they do not typically hear from.*

The proactive phone call, by definition, is a positive conversation. You will ask about the customer's family and life. You will tell the customer you were thinking about her. You will tell her it was important to you to connect. And then you will ask her what she is working on that you might be able to help her with.

The customer will react to this positively. *Nobody will ever tell you, "No, I don't want you to make my life easier right now."* You will feel good about these conversations. You will enjoy an infusion of positivity. (The customer may say to you, "Nobody really calls me like this, when nothing is wrong.")

And then, *the customer will tell you what else they'd like to buy from you.* Either on this call or in a future conversation, additional business *will* come.

You will be rewarded for your proactive efforts. First with a warm, feel-good conversation. Then with additional sales. And then with more money for you and your family.

You will feel pessimism drop and optimism build. You will feel cynicism fall, and you'll experience some gratitude seeping in.

And so, it is the very sales-growing action of proactive phone calls—and, critically, the quick wins that will result from them—that will extract you from your damaging reactive selling mindsets and behaviors. In Chapters 19–24, I lay out the different kinds of customers and prospects you can call proactively, including language and scripts.

In the next chapter, I'll compare the telephone to other pathways of communications in sales, but basically: the telephone will revolutionize your selling. The telephone will change your life.

5-MINUTE
SELLING SUCCESS

"I made a proactive call and asked reverse *did you know* questions [author's note: these are covered in Chapter 26] about what else they need from us. They were ordering 100 water meter padlocks and 200 keys from us, and on this call they added 200 more padlocks and 800 additional keys! That's double the padlocks and quadruple the keys. Awesome!" —Marc R., outside sales, distributor.

CHAPTER 7

Comparing Your Proactive Communications Pathways

The telephone is the best communications pathway for growing sales
quickly because you can make
lots of calls to many customers
and prospects quickly—far more
than in-person visits.

In sales growth, email is only a tiny bit better than doing nothing at all. Here are the communications types, from least effective to most effective:

MOST Effective Sales Growth Communications

In-Person Meeting

Telephone Call

Text Message

Email

LEAST Effective Sales Growth Communications

Silence

Let's discuss these communications briefly, in order.

In-Person Meetings

Of course, these are best, but they also require the most time.

Nothing can replace *seeing* the person, and his body language, in his environment. Meetings also have the gigantic added benefit of being able to see your customer's warehouse, if you are in this kind of work. Here *you can observe what else he buys from others, and offer to help with that.* This is a kind of reverse DYK (although you find the products simply by *seeing* them rather than actually asking the question) and a pivot to the sale.

Face-to-face conversations are the Mount Olympus of sales efforts. Nothing is better. However, they do also require the most time, right?

There are only so many hours in a day, and you can only have so many meetings. If you lay out your visits really well, you can maybe do one visit an hour. That's six or seven a day, in a *very* busy day. Most salespeople cannot sustain this kind of grind.

But most of us *can* make six or seven phone calls in an hour.

So, while I absolutely and completely believe that face-to-face is best, it's not always practical for the kind of volume of communications it takes to predictably grow sales.

Telephone Calls

The telephone is the most valuable and important tool in the 5-Minute Selling System.

Calls are an excellent pathway for communicating with customers and prospects because they're personal, direct, and rare, and they can be done rather quickly. In this book, we're talking about calls that last just a few minutes.

Calls let us hear tone of voice. Emails do not.

Calls let us use silence, which lets the customer think. Email provides for none of this.

Calls let the customer hear our voice. Email lets the customer see our text, the same as everybody else's text. The competition who emails is not nearly as good as us, but their emails look exactly the same as ours!

Calls elevate us above the playing field. Emails pulls us down and make us like everybody else.

Text Messages

Many of my clients and audience members are surprised when I state that text messages are a far more effective method of communicating with customers and prospects than email.

Why? *Because it's disruptive and active, while email is totally passive and in the background.* A text message lands on a customer's cell phone, while email lands in a customer's junk folder. Some text messages even tell us when the customers have read them!

Text messages will get a response far more frequently than email. Even on evenings or weekends.

Think about your own phone: if a text message pops up on our phone, we read it no matter what time of day it is. And if it's a friend or family member or colleague (and *many* of your customers think and feel this way about you!), we reply to the text!

If you have a "cell phone relationship" with some of your customers, you should absolutely utilize text messages. It will be helpful to the customers and also to you.

Email

We have arrived at the least effective pathway for communicating with customers and prospects. This is a very difficult medium to use in sales growth. It comes with myriad problems.

We don't know if our email arrived in our customer's inbox. If the email did land, we don't know if they *saw* it.

If they saw the email, did they *read* it, or just the subject line? Did they *click* on it? We don't know.

If they read it, why didn't they *reply* to it? Do they not care about this? Or are they simply busy?

Maybe they are mad at us. Did we make a mistake? Have we lost the customer altogether?

Welcome to email, where nothing is known and little is sold.

THE ONLY TWO ACCEPTABLE USES OF EMAIL IN SALES

There *are* two specific scenarios where email can be useful in the 5-Minute Selling System.

1. *To Schedule Phone Calls*

I have found it acceptable to get calls on the calendar using email. These work best when the emails are very brief and to the point. "I'm writing to follow up on our last conversation and continue our discussion. I can talk on Tuesday or Thursday. What's better for you to connect by phone?"

Assuming you are emailing people who know you, emails like this fill your calendar. Think about sending three to five a day. You'll probably get at least one call from this set of emails.

Want more calls? Send a few more scheduling emails.

That said, as per the effective communications list earlier in this chapter, text messages are actually a better way to schedule your calls, if you have that kind of relationship with your customer.

2. *To Follow Up on Quotes or Proposals*

In Chapter 28, I lay out a simple way of following up on quotes and proposals with three specific communications.

These quick follow-ups can be sent by email. They would be more effective by phone, of course, and also by text message. But email is a fine way to follow up on previous quotes and proposals.

If you can send them systematically—and, critically, track these communications (see Chapter 12)—you will close significantly more quotes.

AND SO, WE FOCUS ON THE TELEPHONE

When analyzing the ratios of effectiveness versus time commitment, the telephone wins, and it's not even close. This is why there are six chapters in this book about eight different kinds of people we can call and what to say to them.

This is why the telephone is your key for fast and significant sales growth.

The telephone will feed your family. The telephone will set you free. And the text message will be helpful too!

5-MINUTE SELLING SUCCESS

"I got a call from a new CEO of one of our suppliers the other day, and he called me on my cell phone. That's the first time anybody has ever called me for business on that damn thing! We had a great 20-minute conversation, and I increased my order with them, adding two additional new products. It was nice to catch up!" —Jeff K., CEO, commodity distributor.

CHAPTER

8

THE KEY MINDSETS TO FUEL YOUR SALES GROWTH

Mindset fuels our behavior, and we cannot outsell our mindset.

When you start communicating intentionally and proactively with the 80–90% of your customers who are happy but quiet, you will find your mindset shifting from positions that actively sabotage your selling to those that actively catalyze it.

Mindsets fuel our behavior. We cannot outsell or outperform our thinking.

If we *think* that our customers dislike us, and *here comes another annoying customer*, then our sales will reflect this thinking. Conversely, if we believe our customers are lucky to have us (and they are) and that we are helping them a great deal (and we are), then we'll also sell accordingly.

Either way, you need to sell, and I'd suggest that the latter position will make you a lot more money than the former.

One of my favorite quotes, which I use in many places in my work, was spoken by Henry Ford:

Whether you think you can, or you think you can't, you're right.

I think this is one of the best things ever said.

Let's say you have a difficult phone call coming up with a customer who you know is angry. You have two choices:

The first option is the reactive, exasperated, fearful, cynical one: "This call is going to be awful. This guy hates me, and I'm not a big fan of his either. Great! Here it comes!" How's that call going to go? It will be as awful as reading that quote feels!

The second position is the optimistic, confident, positive one: "I know he's displeased, but I'm going to try to help him as much as I can. I'll do my best, and then I'll move on to helping others."

Same call. Same customer. You have to talk to him either way.

You might as well *think you can.* You might as well come into it with a mindset that's helpful for dealing with this person *and also the rest of your day.*

This is the power of our mindset when it comes to systematic, proactive selling.

It is the core. It is the fuel. It is the catalyst.

THESE MINDSETS CAN BE LEARNED AND DEVELOPED BY TALKING TO YOUR HAPPY CUSTOMERS

Assuming you have worked for some years in sales, you are coming into this process with established mindsets. On the continuum between positive and negative, you occupy a position that is typical for you. You tend toward either optimism or pessimism, but your position tends to be consistent. Your thinking tends to gravitate toward confidence and boldness, or fear and meekness.

But I want to be clear: *your mindsets are neither fixed nor permanent.* You can absolutely shift your thinking.

Martin Seligman's seminal work on this matter, *Learned Optimism*, establishes with detailed research that we can learn to be optimistic instead of pessimistic. *We can teach ourselves how to see the positive instead of the negative in a situation.*

And I am arguing strongly here that proactive phone calls with customers— as discussed two chapters ago— will take you there.

These mindsets can be developed, and you do so by talking intentionally and proactively with your happy, quiet customers.

THESE MINDSETS ARE CONTAGIOUS

Negativity is contagious, but so is positivity. Pessimism is contagious, but so is optimism.

If you bring your customers positivity, it will impact them in a good way. Meanwhile, everyone else affects them in a bad way.

You should know that if you bring your customers the mindsets and attitudes detailed in this chapter, you will be one of the only people in their lives to be doing so. And people will pay good money for these rare— nearly extinct— outlooks.

KEY MINDSETS THAT WILL FUEL YOUR SALES GROWTH

Optimism

Most humans tend to be pessimistic— which means most salespeople are, too. All around us, there is pessimism.

Turn on the television news: pessimism. Listen to our politicians for two minutes: pessimism. And negativity. And the end of the world. Right?

Optimism is a rare commodity.

It is *exceedingly* rare in your customers' lives. Remember, they only call their salespeople when there is a problem.

And customers also only hear from their sales reps when there is a problem. Nobody calls anybody when nothing is wrong. Nobody calls anybody with positivity. Because positivity is not urgent.

Bring your customers optimism, and you'll be one of the only ones. This will make you singular to them.

People *want* optimism in their lives. Bring it to them, and they will thank you with their money.

Enthusiasm

I define *enthusiasm* in sales as positive, joyful energy for helping customers and prospects. The dictionary definition for *enthusiasm* adds an excellent word: *interest.*

We must be interested in helping the customer. We must care about the customer.

Enthusiasm is rare in the business world. Among your sales competition, it's basically non-existent. This is because most salespeople answer the phone, get yelled at, get beaten up on price, react to urgent matters, or solve problems all day.

This is a very difficult environment in which to be enthusiastic.

Enthusiasm will help you make proactive calls. Enthusiasm will help you follow up on quotes and proposals.

Enthusiasm will help your customers feel great about hearing from you— because everybody else brings them problems and negativity. But you bring them enthusiasm.

That's a rarified position. Actually, in your customer's life, it's a singular position.

Confidence

Who would you rather buy from: the confident salesperson or the fearful, meek one?

Confident salespeople know how to help their customers and are proactive about it. They say: *"Why don't you let me help you with that? I want to sell you that."* Meek, fearful salespeople don't want to bother customers, so they don't even call.

Confident salespeople are present and communicate to their customers that they care. Meek, fearful salespeople don't want to take their customers' time. They think, *"If they need it, they'll call."* This thinking has significantly grown sales *never*.

Confident salespeople offer additional products and services (by asking DYKs), and they ask the customers what else they need that they can help with (rDYK). Meek salespeople fulfill the customer's request and nothing more.

Confident salespeople actively un-niche the customer: *"I know they're buying things elsewhere that I can help them with. Now let's figure out what that is."* (How do you figure it out? By asking! "What else are you buying elsewhere that I can help you with?" This is the rDYK question.)

Confidence is proactive. Fear is reactive.

And since we've established that proactive selling is the key to predictable, significant sales growth, I think you should choose confidence!

The positive conversations will fuel your confidence. The quick wins will develop it.

Your success will lead to more success, which will lead to more confidence. A righteous, joyful circle of success and confidence! It's much better than the vicious circle of reactivity we've discussed.

Gratitude

Study after study finds that grateful professionals succeed more than those who lack gratitude. And, interestingly, it's gratitude that makes us successful, not the other way around.

This means if you weren't grateful on your way to success, you will not magically become grateful when you attain success. You will be successful (temporarily), but you won't appreciate it—because you didn't appreciate or give thanks for your journey to it. And your "stay" at the successful place will be brief and fleeting.

It's important to be grateful for the journey.

We must be grateful even for the difficult calls, because they bring us closer to the happy, successful calls. We must be grateful for the rejections, because they bring us closer to the successes. We must be grateful for the process.

You can be sure that the 80–90% of your customers who are happy and quiet are grateful for *you.*

And, of course, we should be actively grateful for the obvious things:

- That our customers trust us enough to help them. So let's not take that away from them.

- That we have customers who need what we sell. So let's be present and show them that we care.

- That we are among the best in the world at what we do. So let's share that incredible value with people who can pay us.

- That the amount of money we make is determined only by how hard we work and our perseverance.

Seriously, how lucky are we?

This brings us to the final critical mindset.

Perseverance

Most successful salespeople have experienced thousands of failures and rejections. I know I have.

So what? It comes with the work. When trying to build something interesting, failure always precedes success.

A middle-aged man recently said to me, "I've never failed at anything." And I immediately thought, "This means you haven't tried anything interesting."

Failure is part and parcel of doing challenging things. And selling is certainly challenging.

The job is to keep doing the right things (communicating proactively) in spite of the rejection. Even when it's not going well.

Keep doing the right thing. Because this is what your family deserves. And it's certainly what your customers deserve. And we know that if you do the right things enough times, eventually the success ensues.

In baseball, even if you hit the ball perfectly, it often flies at a defender and is an out. But players know that if they hit the ball the right way *enough times*, eventually the hits come.

It's the same in sales. Make enough of the right communications, and eventually, the sales will come.

In baseball, you go to the Hall of Fame if you fail 70% of the time. In sales, we fail much more than that.

I run a $3 million consulting practice by myself. Most of the prospects I talk to about possibly working together do not become clients—but the right ones do.

In sales, if you have been rejected eight times, a ninth rejection is literally no worse. It's the same. You had no sale, and you still have no sale. So who cares?

Keep trying to help. Keep trying to add value. Keep communicating.

Eventually, you'll find the right fit. Eventually, the money comes.

It always does—if we do the work.

5-MINUTE
SELLING SUCCESS

"Alex, you're right that we only talk to our customers who have problems. It's so refreshing to spend time with the ones who don't have a problem. I'm having *nice* conversations every day now, and it helps me understand what a difference I make. I'm happier at work and happier at home." —Jodi C., customer service, building products manufacturer.

CHAPTER

9

START NOW, AND AND IMPLEMENT CONSISTENTLY

For sales growth, the system is far more important than the individual actions, because it demands consistent repetition over time.

Myclient organiza-
tions average 10–20% new sales from this work. Individual
salespeople often double or even triple their personal sales.

What is *most* responsible for this kind of consistent, predictable growth?

Surprisingly, not the actual proactive actions. It's not the
proactive call that will double your sales. It's also not suggesting another product or service for your customer. And it's
not asking what else they need.

It's not doing any *one* of those actions. *Rather, it's doing
those things consistently and repeatedly over time that will grow your
sales significantly.*

The system is far more important than the individual
effort. Why?

Because one DYK question to a customer won't revolutionize your business, just as one day of eating healthy will
not get you to your goal weight.

One proactive call to a prospect won't generate significant new additional income, just as one day of jogging will
not get you ready for the marathon.

One quote or proposal follow-up will not change your life.

But doing these things repeatedly, over time, in quantity, will change everything.

Another way to say this is that *the system* is far more important than the individual actions.

WHY THE SYSTEM IS SO MUCH MORE IMPORTANT THAN THE ACTIONS

In sales growth, the system trumps the individual actions because it creates quantity and takes timing off the table. This is an incredibly important concept to understand.

If you only communicate rarely, you are at the mercy of timing. That is, if the customer doesn't need the additional product or service you are offering *at the exact moment you are offering it* (and the odds of this are quite long, right?), you will not get the sale.

Because they only hear from you sometimes, if the customer doesn't have the itch at the moment you are offering to scratch, then you will not get the business.

But if you communicate systematically, and the customer hears from you repeatedly and consistently over time, you don't care when it itches. You are placing a back-scratcher on the customer's desk with your name on it. And when the itch comes, he will pick up the back-scratcher, see your name, and call you.

When you communicate systematically, it doesn't matter *when* they need something. Because when*ever* they need it, you're going to be the one who is in front of them.

Not the competition. You.

And yes, five minutes of daily proactive effort is enough to do this.

The most successful
people start a lot.

THE START IS THE SECOND-MOST-IMPORTANT THING

If consistency and repetition of proactive communications activities is the single most important element in successful sales growth, *starting them* is the second-most-important element.

The most successful people start a lot. They take action.

They begin *before* they are perfectly ready, because they will never feel like they are perfectly ready. We'll discuss this in the next chapter.

They begin, and then they evaluate their success. They assess what's working and double down on it; they observe what's not generating results and edit those efforts. If they're still ineffective, they replace those efforts.

Part 3 of this book details 16 proactive communications actions that will grow your sales. But I'm asking you to *start* your proactive communications before you even get there.

5-MINUTE SELLING SUCCESS

"I learned that it's okay to start first and make it better as you go. It's even okay to start when you don't even know exactly what to say, or what to write down on the tracker. The most important thing is to communicate with our customers. Just communicate. And that's what we're doing, and it's going great. We're making more money every day." —Michael J., vice president of sales, large national service company.

CHAPTER
10

YOUR WINS WILL COME QUICKLY

Statistically, we know that one out of every five DYK questions eventually results in a new sale.

Ask five, get one new sale. Ask 5,000, get 1,000 new sales.

Y ou will find that the wins in this work come quickly. That's because the more people hear from us, the more they buy.

And when you start your 5-Minute Selling effort, your customers and prospects will hear from you much more than they are now.

Success will come quickly.

We know, for example, that 20% of DYK questions turn into new business (see Chapter 25 for all the details on this technique).

If you sell products, you'll ask about five different products, and one will turn into a new line item. If you ask about 50, 10 will turn into business. And when you ask 500 DYK questions, 100 will result in new sales.

The percentage with quote and proposal follow-ups is the same. Twenty percent of outstanding quotes and proposals close when you follow up on them in the manner I lay out in Chapter 28.

This means one out of every five quotes and proposals you follow up on will close, usually on the spot, or in very short order after your follow-ups.

So, do these things, and the money will come. These quick wins will motivate you to take more action. They will encourage you and inspire you. They will help your customers, and they will help your family.

But the close is not the only "win" that counts here.

Let's look at the entire list of successes that come flooding in when you do this work.

NEW CLOSED SALES

Yes, as I've laid out, you will close new business quickly. Even my clients with long sales cycles (companies like engineering firms, which sell large projects over a long period of time; and steel distributors, which need to move their prospects away from their current suppliers over many months and sometimes years) find that quick new add-on business occurs early and often.

Actions that generate these new closed sales: DYK questions; rDYK questions; pivoting to the sale; quote and proposal follow-ups.

NEW OPENED SALES

You will find yourself opening up a plethora of new opportunities that did not exist before. You will be stuffing the top of your funnel with high-quality opportunities, which will have a high likelihood of closing. You will begin discussions about new products, services, projects, and initiatives that weren't on the table before.

Actions that generate new opened sales: proactive phone calls; DYK questions; rDYK questions; referral requests.

SALES PROGRESSED TOWARD A CLOSE

You will actively be moving your open opportunities toward a close. Your follow-ups and proactive communications will demonstrate to your customers that you are *interested* in their business. You will move people through your funnel actively and efficiently. You'll be present and engaged, and the competition won't be. In turn, your customers will reward your interest with their business.

Actions that progress open opportunities toward a close: proactive phone calls; pre-quote and pre-proposal follow-ups.

BRAND-NEW CUSTOMERS

Your 5-Minute Selling System will create brand-new customers. By communicating with prospects who know you (not cold calls), you'll be expressing your desire to help them, and in the process, you will impress them with your interest and care. They will see that life with you is better than life with the competition. And they'll dip a toe in the water with you and make a first-time purchase. Of course, a first-time customer is only one purchase away from being a repeat customer.

Actions that create new customers: proactive phone calls; DYK questions; rDYK questions; pivots to the sale; quote and proposal follow-ups.

NEW PROSPECTS

You will uncover new prospects with work, as well. You will create interest where previously there was none. Here, you will be building up the group of interested prospective customers who are not even in your funnel yet. These are pre-funnel prospects. You'll build them in relatively short order, and it won't take them long to actively start discussing buying from you. Because you will be in front of them, demonstrating your interest.

Actions that create new prospects: referral requests; sending high-value weekly emails.

THE INCREDIBLE POWER OF REPEAT PURCHASES AND REPEAT CUSTOMERS

When you sell a new product to a customer for the first time, they are only one purchase away from buying that product repeatedly. And because you are very good at what you do, most of your customers buy from you repeatedly.

Then, you can go about adding the *next* product that will be purchased repeatedly, and the *next*. And all these first-time purchases become *compounding repeat purchases*. A new product sold to an existing customer is gold raining down from the heavens for us salespeople.

When you add a new customer who buys from you for the first time, you are similarly only one sale away from this customer becoming a repeat customer. Of one product. And then another. And then a series of products. Then all you have to do is calculate how often a customer typically buys from you (do they need this product daily, or maybe weekly?) and do the math.

So, essentially, this work we're engaged in is stacking repeat purchases from repeat customers on top of each other.

A repeat customer is the best insurance policy you can possibly have for your future. And your 5-Minute Selling program creates them systematically.

5-MINUTE SELLING SUCCESS

"I asked a bunch of *did you know* questions and sold my customer a series of accessories this week when they came in to buy a water heater. This added $150 to their water heater purchase. But they buy a water heater three times each week. This is, as you drilled into us during the workshop, 150 times per year. Which makes it more than $22,000 of new sales this year. Next, I'm going to add more new products for *this* customer, and guess what? I'm asking a ton of *did you know* questions to *all* my customers. I want the $22,000 over and over again." —Thomas D., counter sales, wholesale distributor.

PART THREE

IMPLEMENTATION

CHAPTER 11

FIRST PLAN YOUR CALLS AND FOLLOW-UPS FOR THE WEEK

Not only does quickly planning who to call and follow up with inform you *who* to call during the week, but the list itself serves as a reminder to make the calls. *Seeing* it helps us take action we might otherwise not do.

Effective, proactive selling begins by planning who we will call and follow up with.

Because we spend our days reacting to incoming problems and urgencies, we don't really end up calling customers and prospects—unless *we* have an emergency to communicate to *them*. Proactive calls from salespeople to customers and prospects—when nothing is wrong—rarely occur.

I think the main reasons for this are:

1. We are very busy reacting. It's not like we're sitting around doing nothing. We're busy.

2. We don't know who to call. *We have no tool to tell us who to call proactively.* Email doesn't tell us.

Our address book doesn't tell us. It's just a list of names and numbers, but it doesn't tell us *who* to call.

Even our CRM system rarely tells us exactly who to call, because most CRM data is not perfectly entered and completely up-to-date at every moment. It's not up-to-date because the salespeople maintaining it are, you know, solving problems.

So, because nothing tells us who to call, when we have a free minute in between incoming customer issues, we don't run to the phone. Because we don't know who to dial.

USING THE PROACTIVE CALL PLANNER

5 MINUTE SELLING — PROACTIVE CALL PLANNER

My Best Customers Who Can Buy More	Customers Who Used to Buy but Stopped

My Smaller and Medium Customers Who Can Buy More from Me	Customers Who Recently Received Products or Services — Follow Up

Customers I Haven't Talked to in Three Months or More	PROSPECTS I Am Having Active Buying Conversations With — Follow Up

PROSPECTS I Once Talked to, but They Did Not Buy — Follow Up	PROSPECTS I Know Are Buying Elsewhere

The issues I just described are why I created this simple planner.

I want you to write some names in it for three minutes on Sunday or Monday for the coming week. Not 30 minutes— 3 minutes.

You can write 5 to 10 names easily in 3 minutes—especially if you reference some sources of customers and prospects. And you should get help. This isn't a test of memory: it's a quick routine of formulating a good list of who to call proactively. To be prompted for the names of people to call, go to your

- Notes on your computer or phone
- Notes in a notebook
- Past emails
- Address book
- Customer Relationship Management (CRM) system
- Your customers' order history
- Your old text messages

Now write down as many names as you can in three minutes.

Quantity is the goal. We don't need perfect names; we need names of people we can help. We need names of people who can buy (more) from us.

Write them in any category that they fit into. They can *all* be in a single category, or you can have a name in *every* category.

It doesn't matter. Just write down people you can call.

And I want to emphasize: write the names of humans on these lines. You can include the name of the company if you'd like, but make sure every entry has the name of a person.

This is because we sell to people. We build relationships with people.

Write down the names of people.

NOW, FILL OUT YOUR FOLLOW-UP PLANNER

While the call planner helps you think of people to proactively call, the follow-up planner gets your mind focused on *opportunities*.

WEEKLY
FOLLOW-UP PLANNER

Week of (Date):

Customers with Pre-Quote or Pre-Proposal Opportunities to Follow Up With	Customers With Quotes or Proposals to Follow Up With	Current Customers Who Can Buy More Who I Can Follow Up With (And What to Offer Them)

I designed it to help you think of the three major kinds of opportunities most salespeople have:

1. Customers with pre-quote or pre-proposal opportunities
2. Customers with quotes or proposals
3. Customers or prospects who can buy more, and what to offer them

Is there a bit of overlap between the two planners?

Sure, but that's okay, because they orient you toward the goal (listing who to reach out to about more business) from different perspectives.

Here, too, write down 5 to 10 names in 3 minutes. That's it. If some names repeat across the two planners, that's okay.

KEEP THESE PLANNERS WHERE YOU CAN SEE THEM THROUGHOUT THE WEEK

Now that you have some names of people written down, keep them in front of your eyes. On top of your desk, or on top of the pile of papers. Pin them to your bulletin board. Keep them as the front page of your clipboard if you carry one.

I want you to see them many times throughout the day.

It's interesting: these planners are lists of names. But they have an even more important purpose than reminding you *who* to call. Their job is to remind you to *make the calls.*

Their job is to jog your memory. Consider it a proactive call stimulus.

Otherwise, outbound calls are kind of out-of-sight and out-of-mind, right? Because our phone is ringing off the hook. Who has time to *make* calls, or even think of them?

These planners can help you remember to do it.

Now, Communicate

Now it's time to pick up the phone and make the calls. Remember, the best time to make proactive calls is in the morning—first thing, if you can.

It's time to make your follow-ups by phone or text or (worst) email. It's time to be active and present.

It's time to implement the 16 actions detailed in this part of the book. It's time to show your customers and prospects that you care.

5-Minute Selling Success

"It was a good week! On Monday and Tuesday, I made several pre-quote follow-up calls on a bunch of change orders with a client of mine. He then asked me to send the quote, which I did on Wednesday. On Thursday, I followed up on that quote, and we tweaked a couple of things. On Friday, he signed off on them—it's $65,000 worth of change orders. I also made a bunch of proactive calls this week and uncovered a $110,000 opportunity with another client, which I am writing the proposal for now." —Mark W., project manager, service company.

CHAPTER

KEEP A QUOTE OR PROPOSAL TRACKER

Among my clients, implementing a quote tracker has doubled and even tripled previous close rates. This is one of the highest-impact, fastest-acting changes you can implement.

I work with sophisticated, successful companies. Many generate in the hundreds of millions of dollars in annual sales. These are companies that have been successful for generations. Their customers have been with them for decades.

They do exceptionally good work. They build strong relationships. They deliver on time. They solve problems at a world-class level.

And, amazingly, many of them do not keep a quote or proposal tracker. Prices are quoted company-wide and are not systematically tracked or recorded.

At far too many companies, quotes are not entirely and systematically captured in a single place. Far too many salespeople do not have a list of quotes or proposals to reference and follow up on.

And to be clear: I realize most people track some of their quotes and proposals. We remember some. We write some down. Sometimes.

I'm suggesting that you *write down all of your quotes and proposals in one place.* You can establish a minimum dollar value of tracked quotes if you wish. But as soon as a price surpasses that point, it gets added to the tracker.

This is one of the highest-impact things you can do for your sales work.

HERE'S YOUR QUOTE TRACKER

QUOTE TRACKER

Quote Date	Quote #	Customer / Prospect Name	Products / Services	Amount $	Follow-Up 1		Follow-Up 2		Follow-Up 3		Week of (Date):
					How	When	How	When	How	When	

Write down the date, the quote or proposal number, the customer or prospect, and what's being priced. Then, there is room to track three follow-ups and columns to record *how* you followed up (email, text, or call) and when.

My experience is that if a sale is going to close, it will do so within three follow-ups. The likelihood of a sale *after* three follow-ups is quite low. Get the language for your three follow-ups in Chapter 28.

What happens when you start keeping an accurate quote or proposal tracker? You start to follow up more, because you know what to follow up on. And your close rate on open quotes and proposals will shoot up so dramatically that it will surprise you.

Consider the following incredible success stories.

A QUOTE TRACKER SUCCESS STORY

A chemical distributor revenue growth client of mine had flat or decreasing sales for years. The average close rate on quotes was around 20%, like most distributors.

There was no tracking of quotes that went out. Reps sent quotes, but the quotes didn't make it onto any list.

This company started to keep such a list: a simple spreadsheet that listed every quote and details about three follow-ups.

One administrative assistant was in charge of maintaining the list: there was one keeper of the list. Every time a quote was sent, this keeper of the log was copied. She'd see the quote and add it to the list.

Every quote from every salesperson went into the log. Every follow-up was entered, as well, with the date and method of follow-up (email, phone, etc.)

What did the close rate do? It jumped to 61%. It *tripled*.

This is a sales miracle, because it was done with no additional work by the salespeople. The number of quotes going out did not increase. But the number of follow-ups skyrocketed.

"It's an incredible result," said the owner of this business. "It hurts to think about how much money we were losing all these years."

And it's so easy to do.

ANOTHER QUOTE TRACKER SUCCESS STORY

I had another recent client—a large plumbing and HVAC distributor with 30 locations—that did a year-long revenue growth project with me. This company was also averaging around a 20% close rate on its quotes historically.

We did an experiment at one of their locations. The location rolled out an Excel-based quote tracker with the same format as the previous client. They logged the date of the quote, the customer, the product(s) quoted, and three follow-ups with date and method.

This firm decided to log quotes above $1,500 only. Anything lower didn't make it onto the list. (I think this number was actually too high for this business. I would have lowered the minimum to something around $500.)

At this firm, everybody logged in to the shared document and entered their own quotes and follow-up work. Every salesperson would check the list at the beginning of each day and send their follow-up emails. If there were calls to make, they'd make them from the car as they drove from customer to customer.

The close rate? It skyrocketed to 91%! They started to close four times the number of quotes—an absolutely monstrous result.

Why wouldn't you do this?

YOU'VE ALREADY DONE 99% OF THE WORK

Here is what one of the salespeople at this company said: "It just hit me: this is the last 1%."

What does he mean?

"We've already done 99% of the work. We've built the relationship. We've served the customer well. We do what we say we're going to do. The customer asked for a quote. We stopped what we were doing. We wrote the quote. We sent the quote. And then nothing. Then we stopped. With this tracker, we do the last 1%. We do the following up."

"But I'm too busy to write down all my quotes."

So you spend a lot of time fielding inquiries and writing quotes. Too many quotes to track, right?

Don't you want to close more of them? Don't you *deserve* to close more of them? What's the point of being so busy and writing all those quotes if you don't do the simple work of closing more of them?

Close them.

But before you can close most of them, you need to follow up on them. And before you can follow up on most of them, you need to know what they are. Which means you need to track them.

Go to my web site, Goldfayn.com, click on the cover of this book, and download this quote tracker. Then, simply write down your quotes. Type them into the PDF if you wish. But for goodness sake, record them.

Your bank account will thank you.

5-MINUTE
SELLING SUCCESS

"After our workshop, whenever I'm getting ready to get in the car to drive to see a customer, I've started asking our admin to print up a stack of my outstanding quotes. I call them to follow up from the car. (Don't worry, I never touch the phone, it's all done with my voice.) It's crazy; I'm closing almost all of them. The biggest reason they don't say yes is because they got busy. They always say 'thanks for reminding me,' when I call them." —Mike A., outside sales, manufacturer.

CHAPTER 13

TRACK YOUR ACTIONS AND SUCCESSES

Your 5-Minute Action Tracker
will serve as a detailed record
of your success, as well as an
invaluable log of opportunities to
follow up on.

As you move through your week, doing your morning calls, follow-ups, DYKs, rDYKs, and other proactive actions, record your actions and success in the 5-Minute Selling Action Tracker.

ACTION TRACKER

Week of (Date):

Day / Date	Customer / Prospect Name	Proactive Action Code	What You Said	What They Said	$$ E, EA, Q/P, C

Total Opened Business: **Total Opened Annualized:**   **Total Quoted / Proposed:**   **Total Closed:**

Download all the 5-Minute Selling Planners and Trackers at www.goldfayn.com | Copyright 2020 Alex Goldfayn

Record the day and date, customer or prospect name, and codes for the communications you made. The codes you can use are found on this 5-Minute Selling System checklist:

THE 5-MINUTE SELLING SYSTEM

Do any combination of these proactive communications with customers and prospects for five total minutes every day. Record your progress in the 5-Minute Action Tracker.

Proactive Phone Calls	Proactive Communications
✓ Call Your Current Best Customers (PC-BestC)	✓ Offer Additional Products and Services to Existing Customers (DYK)
✓ Call Small & Medium Customers to Make Them Bigger (PC-SmallC)	✓ Ask What Else Your Customers Need or Buy Elsewhere (rDYK)
✓ Call Customers You Haven't Talked to in Three Months or More (PC-3moC)	✓ Follow Up on Pre-Quote Opportunities (PreQFU)
✓ Call Customers Who Used to Buy But Stopped (PC-GoneC)	✓ Follow Up on Quotes & Proposals (QFU)
✓ Call Customers Who Recently Received an Order or Service (PC-PD)	✓ Review Order History & Ask About Products Previously Purchased (OH)
✓ Call Prospects You're Engaged In Active Buying Conversations With (PCPro-BC)	✓ Ask for the Business (Pivot)
	✓ Ask Happy Customers for a Referral (Refer)
✓ Call Prospects You Know Are Buying Elsewhere (PCPro-Else)	✓ Ask Your Customers What Percent of Their Business You Have, and Then Ask for More (%Biz)
✓ Call Prospects You've Never Talked to (PCPro-1C)	✓ Send Handwritten Notes (Note)
	✓ Email DYK Weekly (eDYK)

If you asked a stand-alone DYK, enter DYK in the code column. Then write what you asked about: "Asked about a drip pan." And the customer's response: "Didn't know, bought five of each."

If you asked about four different products, record it as 4 DYK and list each product the customer bought or didn't buy.

If, on a proactive call, you asked three DYKs and an rDYK, and then you pivoted to the sale, your coding is: 3 DYK, rDYK, Pivot. Then write down what you offered, what products the customer brought up for the rDYK, and what the outcome of the interaction was—did they buy? Do you need to follow up?

In the $$ column, connect a dollar amount to your proactive action. Add a letter to each dollar amount:

- E is for the estimated value of the opportunity you've opened up.

- EA is for the estimated annual value.

- Q is for the quoted amount. If you write proposals instead of quotes, feel free to use a P code.

- And B is for booked, or sold business.

So: if you asked a DYK about a product that the customer bought for $50, and you estimate the customer will buy this product monthly, write down B$50 (because *this* order is worth $50) and EA$600 ($50 multiplied by 12 monthly purchases).

If you followed up on a quote worth $10,000 and closed it, write down B$10,000.

But if you asked an rDYK and opened up $2,500 worth of business that you think will be purchased weekly because this customer installs these products at about that rate, write E$2,500 and EA$130,000.

Every time you log an estimated dollar amount (E), I'd like you to also add the estimated annual value (EA). If it feels awkward at first, this will pass. The idea is that I'd like you to connect dollar amounts—which can quickly get quite large and interesting—to your three-second communications.

When you fill up a sheet, add up your total dollar amounts and log them at the bottom. Then, begin your next Action Tracker sheet.

Each sheet contains space for 16 entries. So if you log three communication per day, one sheet will last you the week. But if you log more actively, simply use as many as you need.

Your trackers are a gold mine of new business. Revisit them!

One of the best things about your filled-out trackers? They are full of customers, prospects, opportunities, and product offerings *to follow up on.* A completed 5-Minute Selling Action Tracker itself becomes a follow-up planner!

Revisit the trackers. Review them. They will remind you of what you opened and what you closed.

Together, they are a record of your success, and a list of things to follow up on. They *prove* your success and the great value of the work you've done.

They make it impossible to say, "This doesn't work for me." They make it impossible to say, "My customers don't want to hear from me."

They overcome your own negative self-talk and disarm your personal objections. With success. With wins. With new sales and new opportunities.

5-MINUTE
SELLING SUCCESS

"I love having a system and some accountability in my sales work. It only takes a few seconds to jot it down, and I love having a list of all my opportunities from the week. It also reminds me who to follow up with."
—Charlotte A., inside sales, manufacturer.

CHAPTER

14

What to Do If You Miss a Day

Do not abandon the ship if you pass over a rough wave. If you miss a day of 5-Minute Selling, just catch up tomorrow.

The idea, of course, is to take daily action. But this is real life, and you're a human being. You will get busy. We all will.

There will be days you don't get your five minutes of proactive action in.

There will be days the phone rings off the hook, or you need to drive a long distance, or you're simply too grouchy. It happens to all of us.

What do you do if you miss a day? Is it all over? Do you stop everything?

Is the diet over if you have a bad night and eat a full bag of chips on the couch?

For many people, it is. But that's the incorrect approach. Ending everything is far more harmful than the bag of chips.

Stopping your proven sales growth efforts is far more harmful than missing a single day. Stopping everything instantly turns something that's no big deal into a giant problem.

So what should you do if you can't get your five minutes in?

Try to take a single action. A single DYK question about an additional product or service a customer can buy—even if you can fit it into an *incoming* phone call—would be a proactive action done today.

Then, if you manage to sneak in one proactive action, try to do another one. Bit by bit. Snowflake by snowflake, try to keep your sales growth blizzard going.

But if you can't get a single action in, call it an off day and get back to it tomorrow. Just pick it up again the next day.

Do not, under any circumstances, stop your 5-Minute Selling program. That would be a giant disservice to your customers, and you, and your family.

Just do your best tomorrow. That's the work. Do your best.

Some days we get distracted, and we can't do this proactive work. That's life. That happens. And when it does happen, simply get back to it again tomorrow.

It's not over if you miss a day. You're allowed a bad day. You're even allowed many bad days.

Be good to yourself and your family, and get back on the horse tomorrow.

5-MINUTE SELLING SUCCESS

"I pivoted to the sale (Chapter 30) and asked my client 'Do you need me to write a change order to wrap up the project?" They said yes and awarded me $50,000. I also asked them, 'Can you refer us to be on the approved contractors list?' and now we are!" —Praveen K., project manager, service company.

CHAPTER 15

Yes, You Should Leave a Voicemail

A voicemail lets your customer hear your name and your voice, and this alone will separate you from the competition. They're not leaving messages, because they're not calling proactively when nothing is wrong.

There are eight different kinds of proactive phone calls you can make in the 5-Minute Selling System.

If you aim at one proactive call a day, you will make 260 outbound calls in a year. If you decide to target 2 calls per day, that's 520 calls annually.

You *will* get voicemail. Probably a lot. Which is why I know this work can be done in five minutes a day.

This is a question I get a lot from clients and workshop attendees: **Should you leave a message when you get voicemail?**

The answer is yes. You should absolutely leave a message. Why?

Leave a message because these aren't cold calls. The person you are calling knows you, even if they are not a current customer. We are calling friendlies here.

Even if you "only" leave a message, they will be happy to know you called. And using the language I'll arm you with shortly, you are quite likely to get a call back.

Leave a message because you want a call back. How will the customer call you back if they do not know you called?

A message lets them know. I know it's not rocket science. But there it is: without a message, there is no chance of a return call.

Leave a message because the customer will hear your voice and your name. They'll hear your voice, not the competition's. They'll hear your name, not the competition's. They'll hear your company's name.

It's another demonstration of care. You're demonstrating that you are thinking about them—and the competition is not.

Leaving a message when you make a proactive call, like all of these actions, separates you from the competition, which is not as good as you are.

Leave a message because it will help you sell more. Remember, these are happy customers you don't talk to much. Or they are prospects who know you, and you know them.

A voicemail is another touchpoint with somebody who values and appreciates you. Aren't you happy to get a voice message from a friend or family member (who you like!) who you haven't talked to in some time? I am.

And so will your customers and prospects when you leave your message.

HERE IS WHAT TO SAY IN YOUR VOICE MESSAGE

The language is quite similar to the opening you use when you make proactive calls that the customer answers:

"Tom, it's Alex Goldfayn calling. I hope all is well with you and your family. Listen, I was thinking about you and wondering what you're up to. I've got an interesting update for you, too. If you have a quick minute, give me a call back at this number. Thanks, Tom, really looking forward to catching up."

I timed it as I read this out loud, and it takes 15 seconds to say. Figure another 15 seconds for the phone ringing and outgoing message, and you have yourself a 30-second activity.

Remember, many of your calls will result in a voicemail, so we're not talking about 10 or 20 or 30 minutes. We're talking about 30 seconds.

And even if they pick up, I want you to practice doing the entire call in three to four minutes.

One more thing.

What's the "Interesting Update"?

In the voicemail, I'd like you to tell the customer that you also have something of interest to share with him.

You might focus on something personal. Tell your customer about one of your kid's achievements, or maybe a vacation that you took. A new home? A new car? A development in a hobby you share with the customer? Use your judgment, and pick something interesting.

Of course, you can also focus on the professional. Particularly powerful can be a success story with another customer, which could also help *this* customer. Share a product or service you provided another customer similar to this customer who returns your call. Recount a win.

Or, if the person you left a message for is a prospect, *tell* him about a customer of yours who is similar, and the success they are experiencing.

Frankly, it doesn't matter what you share. Just give them something to react positively to.

Why is this interesting share useful in your interaction? Because other suppliers aren't sharing interesting things with this person. They're sharing problems and frustrations! And *you* will be remembered for calling them without a fire to place on their desk.

They will remember this. And they're likely to call you back. And, before long, they'll likely give you more business.

5-MINUTE SELLING SUCCESS

"I can't even tell you how many times I've called this customer to follow up on the quote. I probably left seven or eight messages, and then talked to him three or four additional times. But he never once told me to stop. Finally, he awarded us the project—$120,000! On that call, he told me, 'Thanks for all the calls; that told me something.'" —Tom G., outside sales, manufacturer.

CHAPTER

16

LISTEN, DON'T TALK

Ask a question, and wait silently
while your customer thinks
about the answer.

Don't interrupt them with nervous
chatter. Don't talk your way
out of a sale.

I want to talk about two kinds of silence in this chapter:

- *Macro-listening*, which is the general approach to a conversation with a customer where you do most of the listening and the customer does most of the talking

- And *micro-listening*, wherein you ask a question and do not speak again until the customer answers your question

MACRO-LISTENING

Recently I was shopping for disability insurance, and my regular agency had me speak with a specialist in this area. I had never spoken with him before. And I have little interest in doing so again.

This is because he talked so much, I have no idea when he breathed. For the first 10 minutes of the conversation, he talked with interruption.

More than once, he asked me a question and took guesses at trying to answer it himself. Once, I actually tried to answer his question, but he talked right over me, bulldozing his way to even more airtime.

This wasn't macro-listening, it was macro-yapping.

The only thing that kept me from cutting off the call was that I like the agency and its owners, and I want to keep my business with them.

You cannot sell successfully if you do all the talking. In fact, in a sales conversation, about 25% of the talking is the right amount.

This means that the customer should be allowed to speak for three-quarters of the conversation. How else are you going to learn about the customer's issues?

How will you even know what to do, if the customer can't tell you what they need?

When you do all the talking, you learn nothing. When you do all the talking, you annoy the customer. And you voluntarily walk away from one of the most effective tools we have as salespeople: *listening.*

Because it's impossible to listen if you are doing all of the talking.

Micro-Listening

Too many salespeople fill silences with nervous chatter, talking themselves right out of additional business. Here's what I mean.

Ask for the business ("When can I expect the P.O.?"), and then do not talk until the customer answers the question. If there is an extended silence, let it be. If the customer gives you "umm" and "uh," let them.

Let them think.

That's what they're doing. They're not uncomfortable. They're not annoyed. They're thinking.

Why would you interrupt them?

Do not talk your way out of a "yes." Too many salespeople do exactly this.

Referrals are another example. After asking for one—
"Who do you know like yourself who would benefit from
working with me the way you do?"—remain silent until the
customer has a chance to consider your request.

You have been thinking about asking for this referral, but
your customer has not been. Ask, and zip it. Count to 100 if
you have to. Do not speak until the customer speaks.

When you talk to your customers and there is silence, they
are not frustrated or annoyed. They are considering your
questions. If you interrupt them, you are interrupting their
decision-making process.

Give your customers time to think.

Like most of these things, the vast majority of salespeople
are not very good at this. So if you can get comfortable with
silence, you'll be way ahead of the competition.

5-MINUTE
SELLING SUCCESS

"I made a proactive call and asked a *did you know*
question about a brand-new product line for us.
The customer set up a meeting for further discussion of the product and actually asked for pricing on
the spot! They said it's more cost-effective than their
current supplier. The meeting is next week, and I'd
put the odds of us getting this deal at 75%. Potential
value: $300,000 annually, and they've been a customer
with us for 15 years." —Syed R., field sales engineer,
manufacturer.

CHAPTER

17

It Will Never Feel Perfect, so Just Take Action

Perfection is only a half-step
from procrastination.

Too much selling action is lost to perfection.

Actually, perfection is a close cousin to procrastination. Because the end result is the same—both are obstacles to action.

An old business coach of mine used to say, *"When it's 80% ready, move, because the last 20% is dysfunctional."*

If I make a mistake of omission in this book and leave something out that I wanted to include, who knows about it? That's right, only I do. So I don't worry about it.

I try to do my best, carefully plan, write, edit, and edit again (with some help from the talented people at my publisher, Wiley), and then I *put the work into the world.* Agonizing over it helps nobody.

Delaying it repeatedly to find just one more error, make one more correction, actually hurts me and hurts you. It keeps *all* of the value in this book from you, because of my own perceived (but not necessarily actual) imperfection.

It's the same in sales.

QUANTITY TRUMPS QUALITY

We've already established that sales growth—and the ensuing great additional value for your customers—occurs when you communicate more with customers and prospects. Therefore, it's the quantity of communications—not the perfect quality of them—that determines sales growth.

In our work, *quantity trumps quantity.*

The communications don't need to be perfect. They merely need to be helpful.

The products and the services need to be much more perfect than the communications. The products and services should be continuously evolved and perfected.

The communications need to be helpful . . . and made. That's the most important thing.

The communications simply need to be made.

YOU'LL NEVER FEEL LIKE YOU'RE PERFECTLY READY

No matter how hard I work on this book—even after the tenth round of editing—I will never get to the place where I feel that it's perfect. And neither will you.

You'll never feel perfectly ready to call your customer, so call them anyway.

You'll never feel perfectly ready to ask for the referral, so ask anyway.

You'll never feel like it's the perfect time to ask your customers about other products and services they're buying elsewhere, so ask now rather than waiting for the perfect moment.

The perfect moment will never come. So stop trying to make it perfect.

Stop trying to wait for a perfect moment that will never come. Simply take action.

Perfection helps nobody, least of all you. Action helps everyone—your customers, yourself, and your family.

5-Minute
Selling Success

"Your advice on perfection has changed my life. I'm a lawyer, and it has always been hard for me to finally send out written material because there is always one last improvement that can be made. When you told me to send it when it's *mostly* ready, it was a huge epiphany for me. That's what I do now with my email, and my engagement letters, and everything else I write. I write it, I review it, and then I just send it. This has saved me time *every day*. It's a huge relief!" —Sameer A., attorney.

PART FOUR

THE 16 PROACTIVE COMMUNICATIONS THAT WILL GROW YOUR SALES

CHAPTER 18

ALL ABOUT THESE 16 ACTIONS

We will be interested. We will be present. And customers will reward us with their business.

Because the competition is *not* interested or present.

Welcome to the first day of your new predictable, sustainable, dependable sales-growing life.

Can five minutes really double your sales?

Five minutes of intentional, proactive communication effort per day can. I've seen it happen over and over again among my clients for years.

Communicating proactively with customers and prospects works so well that you can make plans around the additional money you will take home from the new sales that will come from this.

So what are these five minutes per day all about? What kinds of actions are we talking about?

We're talking about five daily minutes of proactive communications. This means these communications are the opposite of answering the phone and reacting to customers' problems and complaints all day, as most of us do. You still need to do this throughout your day, but now, with your 5-Minute Selling System, you'll infuse these proactive communications into your otherwise reactive day.

THE PILLARS OF YOUR 5-MINUTE SELLING SYSTEM

Here are the main components of your new proactive selling system.

- **You'll call customers and prospects proactively when nothing is wrong**—and intentionally guide the conversation to how (else) you can help. This is because customers tend to only hear from suppliers when there is a big problem. Otherwise, customers very rarely hear from suppliers, and prospects almost *never* get calls from salespeople. We *think* their phones are ringing off the hook, but they are not. Any phone call you make to a customer or prospect when nothing is wrong is an excellent sales-growing proactive communication.

- **You will engage in frequent intentional discussions with customers about additional products and services that they need and buy, but not from you.** They're buying these things from the competition. As you sit and read this, you have customers going and buying things elsewhere that they could be buying from you. A huge part of your five daily minutes will be to systematically discuss these products and services with your customers.

- **You will get closer to smaller and more distant customers.** One of the major outcomes of working the 5-Minute Selling System is that you will spend time talking with customers you don't normally interact with. Most of us have a few major customers and many, many smaller ones. Among these smaller ones are customers who *could* buy much more from you. In fact, they *are* buying much more than they buy from you—but they're buying from others. You will talk to these folks much more.

- **The recipients of proactive communications in our system will almost always be people who know your name.** They are people who recognize you and are pleased to talk with you. They don't necessarily have to be current customers, but even the prospects you will be communicating with should be people you know and who know you. If you think about it, you have *many* prospective customers who know you, and who you know:

- These are people who used to buy, but stopped.

- They are people you have been targeting for some time and have had conversations with.

- These are customers from previous jobs who have not bought from you in your current role.

- **As such,** *cold calls are not a part of our 5-Minute Selling System.* I don't want you to call people who won't recognize you. This is difficult and unpleasant work that *almost never* leads to success. I want to be clear: I am not saying that cold calls have no place in sales. They do. But not in our five daily minutes. You can use other minutes on them if you'd like—but leave our five minutes for the specific kinds of communications laid out in Part 4 of this book.

- **Overall, the fast and simple communications in your five daily minutes will separate you from the competition because they are not doing this work.** Chances are very high that your proactive, relationship-building phone call will be the only one your customer receives that day, and probably also that week. Chances are that your quote follow-up, and your referral request, and your handwritten note (all actions detailed in their own chapters in Part 4) will be the only ones they receive this month—and maybe even this year.

A few more quick guidelines:

- **Can a proactive communication in our system be a text message**? As long as the customer or prospect knows your name and recognizes you, then yes, a text message qualifies. That's because it disrupts your customer's routine and reminds them that you are there to help them. *All* of the proactive efforts in our system are designed to make the customer stop and think, *wow, you're really interested in helping me.*

This is why **email has a very small to non-existent role in our work.** It does the opposite of making you stand out from the crowd, doesn't it? It makes you like everybody else. Let the competition get lost in email. We'll be front-of-mind. For our 5-Minute Selling purposes, let's stay away from email as a selling tool, with one major exception: emails used to schedule phone calls are fair game. More on this in Chapter 7.

■ **Can it be a LinkedIn or Facebook or Twitter communication?** Again, if you want to just be more noise for your customers to wade through, sell with social media. We'll use personal, human relationship-building communications to grow our sales in five minutes a day.

Many of these efforts—like telling the customer about another product you can offer—are three-second actions. A quote follow-up is a three-second action. A pivot to the sale is a three-second effort. A phone call requires a minute or so if you're leaving a message (and we *will* leave messages; more in Chapter 15), and five minutes or so if you connect with the person.

Let the competition email and send LinkedIn messages. Let the competition be forgettable and annoying.

We'll be helpful. We'll be interested. We'll be present. Which is all customers want from us.

In turn, in just five minutes of focused, proactive communications effort, we'll grow our sales dramatically.

5-MINUTE SELLING SUCCESS

"I did a quote follow-up call and received a $48,000 order! The customer thanked me for following up and apologized for the delay. Would I have gotten this order without making the quote follow-up? I don't think so, because I know for a fact that two competitors were calling on them also." —Darren T., outside sales, distributor.

CHAPTER 19

CALL YOUR CURRENT AND FORMER BEST CUSTOMERS

Proactively calling your best customers leads to them un-niching you, and you un-niching them. In turn, they start to buy other products and services, and your business expands.

They're our best custom-
ers today. They are the ones who buy the most. They are the
ones who have been buying from us the longest.

Some of them do not hear much from us. And the ones
who do, tend to talk to us when they call us.

Few proactive calls are made from us to them, because we
are busy tending to the squeaky-wheel complainer customers.

Many of our best customers buy from us on autopilot.
And we sell to them that way, too: they ask, we sell. Very rarely
do we explore what they really need. And what they buy elsewhere. And what they're having trouble getting quoted. And
what's on their wish list.

They've niched us, and we've niched them. *"This is what
I buy from them because this is what they have,"* your customers
think. *"This is what I sell them because this is what they need,"* you
say about these customers.

We don't know how much of their total products and services they buy from us. We don't know what else they buy
from others that they could buy from us.

We don't know much—because we don't talk to some of these customers much. And, amazingly, all they really know about us is what they automatically buy.

So, what do we do about this? First, we need to identify who these best customers are.

List your top 10 customers. Make sure you include the name of the human as well as the company. Humans buy, not companies. We nourish relationships with the people at the company, not the company itself.

Top 10 Current Customers

1.

2.

3.

4.

5.

6.

7.

8.

9.

10.

Rate your frequency of proactive communications with each customer on a scale of 1 to 5. Write your number next to the customer.

Remember, we define *proactive communications* as those made from you to customers. For the purposes of this chapter, we're talking about proactive phone calls, obviously.

A **1** is no proactive calls. You only talk to these customers when they call *you.*

A **5** is for those customers you call regularly for no reactive reason. That is, you call them when nothing is wrong. And you're not calling to talk about existing orders; you're calling to check in, catch up, and ask about what they're working on these days that you can help with.

Got them rated? Now look at your list.

Anyone with less than a 5 rating needs to hear from you. Write them into your Proactive Call Planner.

What should you say to them? Be honest and direct, and be interested. Talk to them like you'd talk to a friend, which is probably how they think about you.

"But if they're my best customers, I'm already talking to them enough, aren't I?"

But how many are you talking to proactively, when nothing is wrong? How many are you calling when you don't need anything and there is nothing urgent to share?

HERE IS YOUR LANGUAGE FOR CALLING YOUR BEST CUSTOMERS

"Joe, it's Chris, how are you? How's everything going this week? Listen, I was thinking that it has been a long time since I've called you without an urgent matter to discuss. You good? How's your family? Do you need anything from us on what we're currently doing?

I'm glad things are going well there."

Now pivot to a rDYK question (see Chapter 26): "Listen, I know you have other suppliers because you've talked about them before. What else do you buy elsewhere that we can help you with? I'd love to handle those headaches for you, our way."

Or ask some DYK questions (see Chapter 25): "I know you've been buying these products from us for a long time, but I wanted to let you know we also have products x and y and z that you probably need. Why don't you buy those from us? I'd like to help you with those."

For most of us, the answer is not many. Or none.

I'm not saying you're not talking to them *at all.* I'm just saying you should try to talk to your best customers *proactively* much more.

They are the ones who trust you the most—which means they are the ones who will most reward you with more business.

Don't take that away from them. Or yourself.

TOP 10 FORMER BEST CUSTOMERS

Now let's think through your *former* best customers. Think about the people at this job, or at previous ones, who were *once* your best customers, but no longer are. This doesn't necessarily mean they stopped buying from you altogether (it could, but it doesn't have to be this way). They could simply be buying less.

Look at previous years' results if it's helpful. These people are hard to think of—because we're not talking to them. They've moved on from us. They used to buy a whole lot from us, but not anymore.

Got them? Let's list them here—again, write down the *person* and the company:

1.

2.

3.

4.

5.

6.

7.

8.

9.

10.

Here's what to say to these folks—again, be forward, direct, and totally honest.

HERE IS YOUR LANGUAGE FOR CALLING YOUR *FORMER* BEST CUSTOMERS

"Hi Joe, it's Chris calling, how are you?! It's been a long time since we've talked. What's the latest in your world? How is your family? Kids good?"

Now, gently pivot to the reason for the call: "Great. You know, I was just thinking that there was a time when you were one of my very best customers. I miss those times! (Laugh.) I'd like to have you back in that position, at the top of my list."

Check their order history: "Are you still buying a lot of x and y product? Because we still sell that, and I'd love to be able to help you with that again."

Ask a rDYK question: "What are you buying elsewhere these days? Give us a chance at that business. I won't let you down. It'll be my top priority to make you happy."

This is a pure, honest expression of your interest in helping this person. There is nothing here to get angry or upset about. They will find it flattering. They will be honored.

"But if they're a *former* best customer, they went away for a reason!"

This may be true, but now it's time to get them back. You're simply saying to this person you were once close with that it's time for you to help them again.

This is a singular communication. *Your customer has nobody else in their life who will say this.* You will be the only one.

They will be pleased to hear from you. After all, you've done a lot of business together. And at some point—maybe right now—you have been extremely helpful to them.

Don't neglect these good people. They value you. They want to buy more from you. Help them give you their money.

5-MINUTE
SELLING SUCCESS

"Did a proactive call to my good client to check in with him, and he mentioned he has two projects that he would like us to be a part of for the design. If I didn't call him, this simply would not have come up. This opportunity can be worth $45,000 to us, and our chances are good." —Clint L., client executive, service company.

CHAPTER 20

CALL YOUR SMALL AND MEDIUM CUSTOMERS TO MAKE THEM BIGGER

Our happy small and mid-sized customers have great potential for growth but hear from us the least.

N ow let's talk about the customers who are not the biggest: the small and medium ones. If our *best* customers don't hear from us often, then the small and mid-sized customers are probably completely bereft of proactive communications from us.

Because if we *do* get a moment to call a customer proactively, who will we call? The biggest, most important ones. The little guys certainly won't be getting our attention.

WHICH MID-SIZED CUSTOMERS TO CALL

So, here is how to think about them.

Which of your medium-sized customers, by volume spent with you annually, can buy significantly more? In fact, which of your mid-sized customers can buy enough additional products and services to graduate into the largest customer size?

List them here:

1.

2.

3.

4.

5.

These are the mid-sized customers you should call.

WHICH SMALL CUSTOMERS TO CALL

Now, let's look at your smallest customers. Some are actually small companies and already buying everything they can.

But quite a few are probably larger companies that are only buying a small percentage of everything they need from you. Everything else, they're buying somewhere else.

Who are these small customers who can buy more from you? List them here:

1.

2.

3.

4.

5.

WHAT TO SAY

Your language is going to be quite similar to what I laid out in Chapter 19. Be open and transparent:

"It has been a long time since we've talked, and it's important to me to connect with you. How have you been? How is your family?"

Now pivot to a rDYK question: "I was thinking about you, and I was wondering, what are you working on these days that I may be able to help you with?"

This is who to call.

This will launch you into a discussion about their projects, priorities, and needs.

You will have an enjoyable conversation, and they will be grateful and appreciative of your effort and attention.

"I barely have enough time to call my big customers. Why should I spend time on the little guys?"

Because today's bit players can be tomorrow's major customers. And the truth is, at least some of them are small because they haven't received enough attention from us to buy more.

A good number of these customers buy a lot more of our product—just not from us. These conversations will help us redirect this business to where it belongs: with us.

Aren't they better off with you? Won't you serve them better than the competition does?

They'll appreciate the opportunity to work with somebody like you, who is better than whomever they are working with. Which, itself, will lead to even more business.

When you communicate proactively like this, calling customers you would otherwise not talk to very much, you are busting yourself out of the vicious, reactive circle of dealing with customers' problems and complaints all day. And you are positioning yourself in the glorious, proactive circle of creating new sales where there previously were none.

5-MINUTE SELLING SUCCESS

"I made a proactive call to a small customer of mine. We hadn't talked for several months. We got caught up, and then he mentioned that he is going after a 100-room hotel project and will call us to get a proposal. I will actually be able to help him structure a better proposal for this project, thereby increasing his odds of winning it, and my odds of getting the ensuing business. Win-win all around." —Wade J., business development, large service company.

CHAPTER 21

CALL CUSTOMERS YOU HAVEN'T TALKED TO IN THREE MONTHS OR MORE

These customers are buying on autopilot, in silence. Let's take the controls and help them more, so they can pay you more.

T his is a fantastic group of customers to call.

They're paying customers. But you haven't talked to them in three months or more—which means they've been buying on autopilot for too long.

They're not calling in. We're not calling them. They're in a weird place—they're customers, but we've kind of abandoned them. They are driverless cars, in motion, with nobody to help them get to where they want to go.

But we know them, and they know us. We know what they buy (if we look), and we probably have a good idea of *what else* they buy elsewhere.

You will find they welcome hearing from you.

And here's the biggest key with these people: if you haven't talked to them in three months, chances are *very* high that they need more products or services from you.

List 10 customers you haven't talked to in three months or more:

    1.

    2.

3.

4.

5.

6.

7.

8.

9.

10.

WHAT TO SAY TO THESE CUSTOMERS

The language for these calls is similar to your other customer calls:

"Mary, it's Joe, how are you? Listen, I know it has been a long time since we've talked, but I was thinking about you, and I wanted to pick up the phone. What's happening? How's your work going?"

At this point, you can pivot to how their buying experience with your company is going:

"Mary, how are we doing for you? Are we treating you well? It's important to me that you're happy."

This is a customer service question, and your customer will be happy to tell you if things are going well or not.

Now, finally, we pivot to more products and services.

Ask your rDYK: "What other products or services can I help with, Mary? What else do you need?"

Now, ask for the business (pivot to the sale): "I'd like to sell that to you. Do you want me to add that to your next order?"

"Isn't this too forward? If they need something, they'll call me, won't they?"

Well, they haven't called in three months, right? So what's going to make them suddenly pick up the phone now?

It's not forward at all to pick up the phone and make contact with a good, consistent customer. It's not forward at all to tell them their satisfaction is important to you. It's not forward at all to communicate that you want to help them more.

You are showing them you are interested. You are showing them that you care.

They will appreciate this, because nobody else is doing it. And then they'll reward you with more and larger orders.

5-MINUTE SELLING SUCCESS

"I made a proactive call to a customer of mine who I haven't talked to in over a year. Isn't that amazing? A full year had gone by! I asked about a product he had previously expressed interest in according to my notes, and he said he wants to see it. He said he was glad I called. This new opportunity represents an estimated $15,000 in revenue." —Frank H., sales, service company.

CHAPTER

22

CALL CUSTOMERS WHO USED TO BUY BUT STOPPED

Tell your past customers that you'd like to help them again.

They'll be impressed. And in my experience, the odds are about even that they'll come back.

Unlike your large, medium, and smaller *current* customers, *past* customers are much harder to think of. In fact, any non-customer is, almost by definition, not in our heads. Especially if we sell reactively, like nearly all salespeople do.

Right now, without any research or references, try thinking of five of your customers who used to buy from you, but stopped.

It's hard to do, right? Why is this?

For several reasons:

1. Customers don't announce themselves when they go away. They simply leave, and we are usually so busy that we don't notice.

2. You are not talking with them, and it's hard to think of any customers beyond those we speak to daily.

3. We don't really think about non-customers as people we can call. Our focus tends to be entirely on current customers: specifically, on those who call us regularly. The squeaky wheels.

So, go now to your lists of customers, your email, your address books, and your list of past orders. Make a list here of five customers who used to buy, but stopped:

1.

2.

3.

4.

5.

HERE IS WHAT TO SAY TO THEM

"Joe, it's Mike, how are you? It has been a while since we talked. I was thinking about you and wondering how you are doing. Is everything going well? How's your family?"

Note: When you tell your customers and prospects that you were (1) thinking about them and (2) wondering about their family, it is impossible for them to be anything but honored by your call. It is not possible to be angry with you. It is not possible to be turned off by your inquiry.

Then, as in all of these conversations, pivot to the business portion of the discussion:

"How's it going without us?" And laugh.

"What can I help with? I'd sure enjoy the opportunity to work together again."

This is a kind of reverse DYK. As always, put it in your own words, but be honest, direct, and genuine.

It's really hard not to be impressed with this approach, this language, and this inquiry. You're saying you miss them and you want to help them again. It's difficult to say no to this.

"But they left. Why would they want to hear from me?"

Because you're expressing an interest in adding value once again. Because you can help them out a great deal.

And, probably, if we compare everything *you* can do for them, compared to what the competition is doing for them, they will be better off with you.

Why did they leave, then? Everyone makes mistakes! (You can tell them this, as a joke.)

And now you are giving them an opportunity to fix their mistake.

It's a chance to get back to where people care about them. To where they are not just a number. To where they will be treated as a friend, if not a family member.

It's a chance to be helped by you. And *that* is a really good place to be.

5-MINUTE SELLING SUCCESS

"I went back to call a customer who used to order from us regularly, but he hadn't given us an order in over a year. I asked him where he's buying now, and he told us it's the other supplier down the street. I told him I'd like another shot at helping him. Guess what? He gave us that shot and placed a $3,800 order. On my next call to him, I'm going ask if he'd like to make this a standing (weekly) order. And I'll start asking for the other products he used to buy." —Alison R., customer service, distributor.

CHAPTER 23

CALL CUSTOMERS WHO JUST RECEIVED AN ORDER

A post-delivery call is a fantastic proactive activity. It shows customers that you care and gives you an opportunity to further expand your business with them.

When is the last time you got a phone call from a salesperson *after* you bought something? It doesn't happen much, does it?

Years ago, I feel like car salespeople used to call shortly after you bought a new car to check on how you were doing with your vehicle. But I have not received a call from anyone after my last three car purchases.

Nobody really calls after the sale to check on the delivery. But we should.

Why? Because it's impressive.

Like almost all of the activities in this section of the book, it shows customers that we care.

It's memorable, since nobody else is making calls like this. It makes us stand out from the crowd.

The competition isn't doing this. And making these calls will separate you from them, and make the customer remember you.

This Is a Customer Service Call

My clients love this particular phone call because it is not a sales call but a customer service call first and foremost.

You're checking on your customer's latest order. You're making sure they're happy and asking if they need anything else from you on that order.

This effort resonates particularly strongly with inside salespeople and customer service people, both of whom take orders for much of the day at many companies.

Which Customers' Deliveries Should You Follow Up On?

Obviously you're too busy to follow up on *every* customer delivery. So, the most effective use of this action is to identify your highest-potential customers who just received an order.

That is, who can buy significantly more? Who is currently buying a lot elsewhere? Who do you *want* to increase business with? These are the customers to reach out to with a post-delivery follow-up.

List your top five high-potential customers who just received an order here:

1.

2.

3.

4.

5.

HERE IS YOUR LANGUAGE FOR FOLLOWING UP ON A DELIVERY:

"Hi Ellen, it's Joe; I hope you're doing well. Hey, I wanted to call and see if that last order arrived okay. Everything go well with that? Do you need anything else from me on this?"

If the customer brings up any issues or questions, address them here.

Otherwise, if they're happy, move on to one of the fast communications:

You can ask a DYK: "I'm so glad things went well, Ellen. Did you know we can also help you with product x and product y just as well as we did here with this one?"

Or ask an rDYK: "I'm glad you're happy, Ellen. Now, what other products or services would you like me to take care of for you?"

Or ask her for a referral: "That's great to hear, Ellen. Listen, I was just wondering, who do you know like yourself who would also benefit from working with me the way that you have?"

"I really don't have time to check on deliveries like this. I'm busy enough just answering the calls."

Well, this is a chance to express to your most important customers that their happiness with you and your company matters. It's also an intentional discussion of additional business. You're making the customer happy *and* raising the possibility of doing more together.

Further, like most of these calls, it will take five minutes or less to make this post-delivery follow-up. If your phone starts to ring off the hook at 9:00 a.m., make this follow-up at 8:30 a.m.

And, as I laid out a few chapters back, you don't need to make a whole lot of these calls to start elevating your sales. One or two proactive calls *of any kind* detailed in this and previous chapters will make a significant impact.

Which means we're talking about maybe one or two post-delivery calls per week to make you stand apart from the competition. And impress your customers with how much you care. And sell them more.

It's a wildly effective use of a few minutes per week!

5-MINUTE SELLING SUCCESS

"I try to make at least one post-delivery call every day now. I really like it because I'm just checking if the customer is good, and they like it because they appreciate knowing that I care. It amazes me how many additional orders they place on these calls. I ask for additional business on every one of these calls, and I'd say I get it on around half of them. I love that!" —Jade R., customer service, manufacturer.

CHAPTER 24

CALL
PROSPECTS

Your prospective customers are currently suffering through the competition. Rescue them.

I n this chapter, I am combining all three common kinds of prospects that we should be making phone calls to. I'd like to talk about them in a way that makes a single chapter most helpful.

There is a great irony in the sales profession: experienced, successful salespeople do not call on prospects very much. We spend nearly all of our time with existing customers.

WHY EXPERIENCED SALESPEOPLE SPEAK NEARLY EXCLUSIVELY TO CUSTOMERS, NOT PROSPECTS

The reasons for this are multitudinous:

1. Current customers call us all day long, but prospects do not. Current customers bring us their orders, questions, problems, and urgent matters. Prospects do not.

2. For experienced salespeople, the vast majority of our business comes from current customers. The repeat orders? By definition, they come from current customers.

3. It's easier to sell to customers than prospects, right? They know us, and we know them. We have a relationship. They have an account. They may have credit with us. It's easier to refill a prior order, or add to it, than to sell an order for the first time.

4. When we go visit our customers in person, we tend to go to the ones already buying, rather than the ones not yet buying. We spend time with the customers who are currently paying our bills, not the ones who might one day pay the bills.

But these things are only true for experienced salespeople: only those of us who have been doing this a long time and have a book of business already.

Salespeople who are newer to the profession do not have a critical mass of current customers yet. They must develop business, and so they do. *They* call on prospects.

As the years pass, and we experience sales success, our ratio of communications to customers versus prospects inverts—mostly because the customers call us in droves. And they take our time.

But in the work of predictable sales growth, we need to make one or two calls a week to prospects as well.

THE VALUE OF CALLING ON PROSPECTS

When you call prospects, you are building your "bench." That is, the customers are your starters.

The prospects are your minor leaguers. The first time they buy, they move to your bench.

When you talk to prospects, you develop your sales foundation. They are your future customers. They are, simply, *your future.*

If you prefer a different metaphor: we must talk to prospects to fill the bottom of the funnel. Working to develop prospects so they progress toward their first (of many) sales is a critical indicator of a healthy business.

HOW DO YOU KNOW WHICH PROSPECTS TO CALL?

As with everything in the 5-Minute Selling System, the only way to know who to call is to spend a minute or two thinking about prospects and writing them down.

Because we spend our days responding to calls from our customers, the names of prospects we can call are not in our heads. *Unless we make time to think about them, we will not think about them.*

As most people tell me, "Your stuff isn't really rocket science, Alex." And I reply: *that's why it works. If it were complicated, busy salespeople would not do it.*

So, here are three types of prospects you can call on.

CALL PROSPECTS YOU ARE IN ACTIVE BUYING CONVERSATIONS WITH

Do you have any prospects you're actively speaking with now? These are people you have open opportunities with, but they have not yet bought.

They may be pre-quote or pre-proposal, or they may have received their pricing already. The key with these folks is that they have not purchased.

List five (or as many as you have, if fewer) here:

1.

2.

3.

4.

5.

HERE IS WHAT TO SAY

This is a follow-up call, essentially, and a pivot
to the sale:

"Tom, I was thinking about you and wanted to follow up on our last conversation. Helping you is important to me. Where are you at on this? I'd love to start
working with you on this."

You're asking for the business. You're demonstrating interest.

Do this, and you have a good chance to get the business or,
at a minimum, progress toward a close.

CALL PROSPECTS YOU KNOW ARE BUYING ELSEWHERE, AND RESCUE THEM FROM THE COMPETITION

These are customers who are currently doing all their business with another supplier or provider.

You know some of these prospects. We all do. *They are suffering with the competition*—because the competition is not as
good as you.

The competition does not return calls immediately, like
you do. They are not available on evenings and weekends,
like you are. The competition doesn't get in a car during
an emergency and drive the product over to the customer
like you do.

And, amazingly, the competition doesn't do what they say they will do. I thought if you were in business, you had to do what you say you're going to do. This is very much not the case. Most people, as it turns out, do not do what they say they will do. They take customers' money and then often do not do what they promised. Nice, right?

If you don't believe me about these things, ask your good, happy customers. The language is: "Can you tell me about what life is like with our competition? What do they do that's worse than us?"

They'll tell you all about it.

Aren't these prospects better off with you? Wouldn't they be better served by you? Wouldn't their lives be easier with you? Of course they would.

Rescue them. Help them.

List five of these prospects here:

1.

2.

3.

4.

5.

HERE IS WHAT TO SAY

Here, I'd like you to communicate a testimonial:

"Tom, I know you're with X Competitor currently, and I wanted to reach out to you. I actually have a customer similar to you. His name is [insert name—of course, not a competitor], and he says that working with us is twice as fast as the competition, and that he can reach us any time including weekends and evenings. Now I'd like to help you this way. Would you give me an opportunity to help you this way? What are you working on these days that I can help you with?"

I've selected two common compliments that are shared by customers in testimonials, but, of course, insert your own customers' testimonials instead of mine. And, also, as I wrote, make sure the customer whose testimonial you are sharing does not compete with the prospect.

Why does communicating testimonials work so well on these calls? Because you are not singing your own praises. Rather, a paying customer is singing your praises.

If *you* said that you will be twice as fast as their current supplier, it would not come off well. It would be awkward and oddly braggartly.

But when the customer says it, there is no way to argue with it. There is no defense. It is simply the truth.

CALL PROSPECTS YOU ONCE TALKED TO, BUT WHO NEVER BOUGHT

In my business, I have many of these kinds of prospects. They are usually folks who have seen me speak at a conference or have been referred to me.

We have spoken on the phone at length about their business and how my sales growth work would be implemented there. Perhaps we've had an in-person meeting. We *may* have gotten to a proposal. But they did not buy.

You have these kinds of prospects, too. They are excellent prospects to reach out to, because they know you well, and you know them well.

I make sure to communicate with them at least every six months, while some priority prospects hear from me quarterly. It's on my calendar to call them.

Every single year, two or three of them become clients. And since I can only work with 8 to 10 new clients per year (because I do nearly all the work myself), they represent a significant portion of my business.

If I didn't call them to catch up every now and then, they would not be clients. And I could not help them.

List five of these prospects here:

1.

2.

3.

4.

5.

HERE IS WHAT TO SAY TO THESE PROSPECTS

"Tom, I hope you are well. It has been a while since we've talked, and I was thinking about you. Where are you at on that order (or work) we talked about? I'd sure love to help you with that."

Like the first set of language, this is a follow-up and a pivot to the sale. You are telling this prospect that they are important to you.

Very few people in their lives follow up like this. You will stand out. And they may well reward you with the business.

"But customers dominate my time. How in the world will I find the time to call these prospects?"

We need to make one or two calls per week to the prospects you wrote down in this chapter. That's between one minute (if you leave a voice mail) and five minutes (if you have a friendly conversation) per call.

Every time one of these prospects buys from you for the first time, they are a half-step from becoming a repeat customer, which is the lifeblood of your business.

And if stacking repeat purchases is the name of the game in sales success, then prospect development and conversation are very important components of your long-term revenue growth.

Prospects turning into customers means a secure and successful future. One or two calls to these folks per week is what it takes. Not one or two per day—one or two per week.

Don't forget about calling your prospects. They are the key to your successful sales future.

5-MINUTE
SELLING SUCCESS

"After your training, I decided to call at least two prospective customers per week. I've kept a list of people I've talked to who didn't buy over the years, so they were easy to find. This was 8 weeks, so I've probably talked with around 20 prospects, because some weeks I managed to call more. I just took a look at my numbers before our call: five of them put in an order with me, and I'm talking to another three of them about a potential order. That's a 40% hit rate. None of the orders are huge, but they're all *first* orders, and I know there's a lot more where those came from!"
—Darren A., outside sales, distributor.

CHAPTER 25

EXPAND YOUR PRODUCTS AND SERVICES WITH CUSTOMERS

The *did you know* (DYK) question is a powerful three-second effort for sales growth.

We assume our customers know everything we do. But they do *not* know. Even if we *tell* them, in most cases, they still don't know.

We recently moved homes, and my wife hired a moving company. For the first time in our lives (and we've now moved four different times), instead of doing it ourselves, we had a moving company pack up the house.

A crew of people descended upon the house. In one day, everything in the cabinets, drawers, and closets was carefully wrapped and placed into boxes, which were loaded onto the moving truck.

The next day, they brought all the boxes to the new house and placed them where my wife directed. There were hundreds of boxes all over the house.

Then they left.

That night, our friends came by with a bottle of wine to welcome us. Looking around at the towers of boxes, my friend asked, "Why didn't you have them unpack?"

"Oh, they don't do that," I answered.

"They do," he said. "They did it for us."

I felt physical pain—because unpacking endless boxes is up there with spending lots of time in the dentist's chair for me.

So I tried to protest weakly: "Well, my wife really likes to put things where she wants them to go."

"They don't put it away, they just unpack the boxes onto counters," said my friend. "And they make the packing paper and boxes go away."

If you've moved, you know that simply disposing of the boxes and packing materials is a big project. And that's *after* the gigantic project of unpacking.

At this point, I simply shouted: "*Are you freaking kidding me?*"

I had no idea the movers did this. They didn't mention it to me. They didn't ask me if I'd like them to do this.

I didn't know!

If they had told me they would unpack our things, I wouldn't have asked how much it cost. I simply would have said, "Yes! Please, please, do it! Unpack the boxes, and make the trash magically go away."

Alas, they didn't tell me, and I couldn't buy this service. Because I simply didn't know.

Here's the question: how much money has this cost the company over the years? How many customers would have said yes, if only they knew?

WHAT ELSE CAN *YOU* SELL YOUR CUSTOMERS?

Right now, as you read this, your customers are buying something from the competition that they could be buying from you.

They would like to buy it from you, because they value your partnership a great deal. You would like to sell it to them, because you'll be helping them more, and they'll be paying you more. But none of that is possible, because they do not know.

The three-second technique in this chapter lets them know.

THE DID YOU
KNOW QUESTION

For my clients, this is the most-used of all the techniques in this book.

My clients have asked millions of these DYK questions over the years. *Millions.*

And in those years, counting the repeat business that has resulted, these questions have generated hundreds of millions of dollars. These questions did that. (Will you ask them?)

We know these results, because they are tracked. The results are tracked.

With a DYK question, you are asking if the customer needs another product or service you offer.

YOU ARE STACKING
REPEAT SALES

If you sell consumable products, or services that need to be used repeatedly, these DYK questions will be incredibly powerful for you.

Because every time you add a new product or service to a customer for the first time, they will probably keep buying it again and again, forever.

Because you are this good. Because they need the product repeatedly. Because nobody wants to go to three suppliers when they can do it all with you. It's more convenient. And you're better.

And so, every time you ask a DYK question and the customer buys, it's another product they will buy frequently, repeatedly, for years on end.

You are stacking repeat orders on top of each other. You are, once more, creating a blizzard.

A blizzard of repeat business. A blizzard of sales growth. A blizzard of money for your family.

HERE IS YOUR LANGUAGE FOR ASKING DYK QUESTIONS

This might be the simplest language in the book. You're just naming products the customer probably also needs, with whatever current product you are discussing with her:

- "Did you know we can also help you with product x?"
- "Do you also need product y?"
- "What about product z?"
- "How are you on product a?"
- "Do you need product b with that?"
- "Should I also add product c?"

So, although this technique is called DYK, you do not have to use the words *did you know*. Just use whatever feels right, and name an additional product this customer probably also needs. The sooner this becomes your language instead of mine, the better it will go for you.

CUSTOMERS ONLY KNOW ABOUT 20% OF ALL THEY CAN BUY FROM US

Just because you tell a customer something doesn't mean they know.

We *think* they know. Because *we* remember everything we say.

But *they* don't remember, because they're thinking about their own problems and products, not ours.

Plus, how many times have you heard *this* from customers: "I didn't know you did that!" And you say, "I *told* you we did this a month ago, and you had the exact same reaction!"

Just because you tell somebody something, doesn't mean they know!

PLANTING SEEDS AND TIME

I'm a gardener. Gardeners know that you cannot plant a single seed and expect it to sprout into a beautiful, strong plant.

You need to plant many seeds, nourish them, take care of them, and invest your time and energy in them as they grow, and then they will reward you with a good, strong plant or two—or more, if you're lucky.

Sales is the same way.

Sales growth is a game of planting seeds and time. You cannot simply plant one seed—or ask one DYK question—and expect it to turn into business.

You need to plant many seeds—or ask many DYK questions—*over time, consistently and systematically,* and you will be rewarded with new business.

That is what the DYK question does: it plants seeds. Many seeds. Over time.

And then they start to grow. And you start to sell more.

ONE OUT OF FIVE DYK QUESTIONS TURNS INTO A NEW LINE ITEM

In fact, we know statistically exactly how many seeds you need to plant.

We know that one in five DYK questions turns in to a new line item added. That's 20%, right?

Ask five DYK questions, and you will close one.

Ask 50, and you will add 10 line items.

Ask 5,000, and you will add 1,000.

I want to be clear—*if you will ask these questions, one in five, on average, will turn into new business.* Not maybe. Not hopefully. This is what *will* happen. This is what has happened for years. All you have to do is ask.

Will you? Will you ask the questions?

"But these are my good customers. They already know everything I have."

Do they? Is that why they say, "I didn't know you did that" so much?

We *assume* they know, but they do not. The reason is that they are not thinking about your products.

You are thinking about your stuff all day long. But the customer isn't. They're thinking about their stuff.

This discomfort is yours, not the customers'. It's your fear talking.

In fact, based on my clients' feedback over the years, it turns out that customers consciously know about just 20% of everything you can offer them. That's it.

This means it's physically impossible for them to buy the other 80% from you. How can they buy it if they do not know about it? *And even if you tell them, it doesn't necessarily mean they know.*

Why would you take away all this value from your best customers?

Share your great value. Help your customers. They deserve to benefit from buying more from you.

YOUR TOP 10 DYK PRODUCTS OR SERVICES

Which additional products or services can you ask your customers about? Superficially, which add-on products or services are they most likely to buy?

List them here:

1.

2.

3.

4.

5.

6.

7.

8.

9.

10.

Now, go and ask DYKs about these products. It doesn't matter that you ask the perfect DYK. You don't need to plant the perfect seed.

You simply need to plant lots of seeds. Just ask lots of DYKs.

5-MINUTE
SELLING SUCCESS

"Asking the *did you know* question has become automatic for me. I think I ask DYKs in nearly every single conversation I have with my customers now. I don't even think about. And I'll ask them rapid-fire, too. If they don't need the first product I suggest, I go to the next one. And the next one. In many of these cases, we end up with a product they are interested in. Now, when I forget to ask a DYK, my customers actually *remind me!* More than once, a customer has said, "Hey, aren't you forgetting to upsell me?" We laugh about it." —Mike P., inside sales, manufacturer.

CHAPTER

26

Ask What Else Your Customers Are Buying from Other Suppliers

This technique, the *reverse did you know* question (rDYK), often makes my clients more money than any of the other approaches I teach.

The rDYK question *asks your customers to name products and services that they need,* rather than you suggesting products with did you know questions.

HERE IS YOUR LANGUAGE FOR ASKING RDYKS

- "What else are you buying elsewhere that *I* can help you with?"
- "What else do you need that we can provide?"
- "What do you buy from those other suppliers that you always complain about? Let *me* help you with that!"
- "What else do you need quoted or proposed?"
- "What other projects do you have coming up?"
- "What are you having trouble getting quoted?"
- "What's next?"
- "What products or services are you having trouble getting quoted?"
- "What's on your wish list?"

WHY DO THESE QUESTIONS WORK SO WELL?

Because we *learn* what else the customer needs. Many times, they will name products and services that we simply didn't know they needed.

Sometimes your customers will simply start *listing* products and services that they need. A veritable laundry list!

5-MINUTE SELLING
SUCCESS STORY

I was with a distributor client's sales team in a follow-up workshop, which I do about 90 days after my clients systematically launch this work, and the attendees were sharing their success stories.

One outside salesperson raised his hand and said he was talking with his customer last week, and asked her, "What's on your wish list?"

The customer thought about it for a moment, and said she would send him a list. It arrived by email five minutes after they hung up.

"How many items were on the list?" I asked.

"Twenty-four," he said incredulously.

"All things she needed that she wasn't buying from you?"

"Yep," he said, smiling.

"How many have you sold?"

"Only 10 so far," he said.

Only! In one week!

"How often will she order them?"

"Most of these products will be sold to her at least weekly," he replied.

Which means, if we calculate conservatively, that this 3-second question will lead to 520 new line items this salesperson didn't have before.

And that's only at the moment. Ten new products, to be purchased repeatedly, until the end of time.

"Get to work," I said. "You've still got 14 products to sell from that list!"

"But my customers need to maintain multiple vendors!"

Many times, salespeople tell me that their customers are required to have multiple suppliers. For some of you, this is true, especially if you work with procurement departments.

Fine, but they can still transfer more products and services over to you and continue maintaining some (but less) business with those other, lesser, suppliers.

Plus, you're better than they are. Ask your customers, and they will tell you this.

Let them figure out how to work with you more. They're really good at accepting help that will make their lives easier.

"Why would my customers tell me about other products they buy? That's confidential!"

Because they value you. Because you have a great relationship with them. Because you help them in amazing ways.

Because of all this, they'd like to help you back.

That's what friends do. They help each other.

It's also what partners do. And many of your customers think of you as a friend and partner.

This is difficult to remember, because you spend your days dealing with customers who have problems and are complaining about them. But always remember, those are just 10–20% of your customers.

The others feel fortunate to be buying from you. And they'd be very happy to buy more from you. This rDYK question allows them to do so.

Let them. Help them more. Make more money.

5-MINUTE SELLING SUCCESS

"I asked a customer what else they need quoted the other day, and she named three products that we carry. I priced them on the phone, and she added them to the current order. It's only an additional $1,800 on this sale, but she will buy this at least every week." —Sarah H., customer service, distributor. [Author's note: "At least every week" means at least $93,600 per year. These small add-ons get interesting in a hurry.]

CHAPTER 27

Looking Back and Selling Forward: Leverage Order History

A customer's order history is a rich list of products and services they probably still need.

Y ou have an incredibly valuable resource at your disposal that few salespeople use effectively. This resource is your customers' order history.

Think of it as looking back and asking forward. You look back at what your customers used to buy and ask if they want it again going forward.

This is a five-second look back and a three-second question forward.

If a customer has stopped buying something they used to buy, it is almost always for one of three reasons:

1. They've moved their business elsewhere.

2. They've forgotten to reorder and risk their inventory running perilously low or running out altogether.

3. Their needs have changed, and they no longer require the product.

So when you ask the question about order history, one of the most valuable outcomes to you is that you will learn why *this* customer stopped buying *this* product. You will learn *why*.

You will find that if a customer used to buy something regularly, but they have not bought it recently from you, the most common reasons are #1 and #2 from my list—either they've changed suppliers for that item, or they've become busy and neglected to reorder.

Either way, you asking about it will impress them. They will be impressed with your interest. And they will appreciate that you *noticed* and *asked* about it.

Many of my clients have brought back significant amounts of business with this technique.

Order History Selling Success Story

It's difficult to pick just one, because I've heard hundreds of these success stories from my client salespeople. Here's a typical one that happened recently.

Mandy, an inside salesperson at a manufacturing company, reported this result: "The customer called to place his order, and I went back to check his order history. I said, 'I noticed you haven't bought [three different products] since September. Do you need more of any of them?'"

He replied: "You know what, we *are* running low on two of them. Thanks for reminding me!"

To her great credit, Mandy didn't stop at a single order. She went straight to the repeat business:

"Do you want me to set up an automatic monthly shipment for all three items, so you never have to worry about running out?"

"Actually, that would be good, thanks," he said.

I asked what the total order amount was. About $800 per product, per month, Mandy explained.

That's $2,400 per month, and $28,800 annually—from a quick look back and a three-second question forward.

HERE IS YOUR LANGUAGE FOR ORDER HISTORY SELLING

- "I was looking back at your order history and noticed you used to buy product x or y. Do you need more of that?"
- "I see that it has been six months since you've ordered product x. How are you doing with that?"
- "Hey Joe, you haven't bought this in some time time. Let me send some out so we can make sure you don't run out."

These questions show customers that you care and that you are interested. They don't have many people in their lives bringing up past orders.

"But these past orders are not what they're calling me about. I don't want to upset them."

Okay, so take care of what they're calling about, and *then* pivot to the order history item. Fill the order they need, and then ask about what they used to buy.

The part about upsetting them? Why? Because you're trying to help them more?

Remember, nobody will ever say to you, "No, I don't want you to help make my life easier today." This is *your* discomfort, not the customers'. It's your fear of rejection and failure and losing the customer.

These are common and understandable fears. But it is these fears that make us reactive.

Operate from a position of confidence that comes from knowing the great value you bring to your customers. Then, behave accordingly: boldly.

5-MINUTE
SELLING SUCCESS

"I checked my customer's order history right before I made a proactive call, and asked him if he needed a refill on a few of the items that he hasn't bought in a while. 'Oh, yes,' he said, 'thanks for remembering that for me.' I wrote the order for around $2,800. Easy money!" —Joe D., inside sales, manufacturer.

CHAPTER

28

Follow Up on Pre-Quote Opportunities

This kind of follow-up is impressive to customers, mostly because nobody else is talking to them like this.

Always remember that the competition only tends to call when something is wrong.

Y ou have open opportu-
nities with customers that are in the pre-quote stage. You've
had the initial conversation about a new purchase, but you
haven't quite advanced to a quote or proposal yet. They're in
your funnel, but they don't have a formal price from you yet.

These opportunities are frequently neglected because following up on them requires us to *remember* them.

We need to stop what we're doing to think about these
and actually follow up on them. They require our active
attention. And because customer problems and urgencies
pour in all day, they're quite difficult to break away from.

So, what's the solution? I'd suggest keeping a list of these
on your Weekly Follow-Up Planner and making your follow-
up communications first thing in the morning.

I don't love email for sales, as you know, but I think email
is a useful tool here: you can follow up on many opportunities quickly with email, early in the day.

> ## HERE IS YOUR LANGUAGE TO FOLLOW UP ON PRE-QUOTE OPPORTUNITIES
>
> "Tom, how are you? I was just thinking about you and those products/services we discussed last week. Where are you at on those? I'd love to help you with that—please let me know if you're ready for a quote/proposal."

You can copy and paste that to five different customers each morning, can't you? If the spirit moves you, you can pick up the phone and call one such customer in the morning.

Make your own routine, but do make the progression of opportunities—the advancement of deals from pre-quote stage to the quote stage—a priority in your 5-Minute Selling System.

PRE-QUOTE OPPORTUNITIES FOLLOW-UP SUCCESS STORY

Several products had come up when John was visiting his customer at his warehouse. The customer said he bought these items but from another supplier, and that he was good for now.

John made a note of this, and to his credit, he called two weeks later to follow up with the customer as a part of his 5-Minute Selling process.

"Last time, we talked about those other products you buy," he said. "I want to sell them to you."

Just like that. Direct and simple.

As John was telling this story in front of sales colleagues during our web call, I asked him where he found the confidence for that simple line—"I want to sell them to you."

He replied, simply, "Because it would be good for the customer, and it would be good for me!"

The customer was impressed and moved one of the products to John on the spot. Within weeks, he had moved two others.

That's three new products, purchased repeatedly, for years and years —thanks to one quick follow-up on a pre-quote opportunity.

"But I haven't even sent the quote yet! There's nothing to follow up on."

The goal is to progress the sale and, above all else, get the business. Sending the quote is not the goal.

So stay present on these (and all) opportunities. You'll find your customer may bypass the quote altogether and just tell you to write it up.

This kind of follow-up is impressive to customers, mostly because nobody else is talking to them like this. Always remember that the competition only tends to call when something is wrong. They bring problems to your customers.

But when you follow up like this, you're bringing the opposite of problems. You're bringing solutions to their problems.

5-MINUTE SELLING SUCCESS

"I scheduled a meeting to review upcoming projects with a client, and he went over five different engagements that they'd need us on in the next several months. I got a status update on each one, as well as our role in each one and the approximate size of each one. There's so much business out there!" —Christine B., client executive, service firm.

CHAPTER 29

FOLLOW UP ON QUOTES AND PROPOSALS

When you follow up on a quote, you are telling customers that they matter to you and that, unlike the competition, you are thinking about them and trying to help them.

In Chapter 12, we discussed the critical importance of an accurate quote and proposal tracker. Now, let's turn our attention to what to do with it.

In this chapter, I will use the terms *quote* and *proposal* interchangeably for easier reading.

Having a log on its own—a *list* of quotes and proposals—won't make us any money. But actively following up on those quotes will generate a lot of easy sales for you.

Being present will make you rich. That's because customers like to either say yes or say nothing.

People don't like to say no, because it's uncomfortable. It doesn't feel good to say no. So they say nothing.

But that's only some of your customers. Some others—*many others*—are silent not because they don't want what you've quoted, but because they got busy. And because they forgot to get back to you. It got away from them.

They want it. And they *need* it. But they won't have it because they got way too busy, and it's not in their mind to follow up.

This is why we follow up. In fact, we should make three different follow-ups, in sequential order.

In this one rare exception of a case, you can send these communications by email. It's okay. In spite of myself, I admit that email is an okay (but far from the best) way to follow up on quotes and proposals.

HERE IS YOUR LANGUAGE FOR FOLLOWING UP ON A PROPOSAL

First, ask if they got your quote or proposal.

Send this quick one-line email within 24 hours of sending your quote: "Joe, did you get that proposal we talked about? I want to make sure it got to you, because these things tend to get picked off by spam filters."

It's a yes-or-no question. It's fast. It's easy. And the customer should reply as a courtesy, likely with some update on what they think of your quote.

Now, if they reply to any of these follow-ups, stop the follow-up and start the closing process. But if you are greeted with silence, move on to the second follow-up.

Your second follow-up tells the customer you're thinking about them and would like to help.

"Joe, I was thinking about you and those products I quoted. Listen, I was wondering, where are you at on that quote? I'd sure like to help you with that."

Here you are establishing that this customer is important to you. And that this order is important to you. And that you wish to help them. And this is really, really rare and impressive.

Do not think that every salesperson in this customer's life is following up with them like this—because the opposite is true. Almost nobody is following up. Almost nobody is being proactive. Almost nobody is communicating that they care like this.

Because almost everybody is afraid.

I repeat: if the customer replies, do not go to the final follow-up. Stop following up, and start closing.

Your third and final follow-up announces to the customer that you've waited long enough!

Look, you've now made three different communications.

The first was the quote. The second was the initial follow-up about whether the quote landed as intended. And then you communicated a third time about how you care about the customer and this order.

If you have not yet received a reply, the customer is simply being rude. They asked you for this quote. You stopped what you were doing and wrote it. You sent it. You followed up twice.

If they are still silent, they deserve that you take it away from them: "Joe, I sent the quote for those products as you asked, and then I followed up twice. I still haven't heard from you. I wanted to let you know that the quote is expiring in 24 hours (or 48, if you wish), and the file is going to close. I hope I can help you on this, but if it doesn't work out, I'm sure we'll come together on something soon. I look forward to hearing from you!"

Take it away!

You will find that some customers will reply to this final follow-up and beg you to please wait—they've simply been much too busy!

Of course, you need an expiration date on the original quote to do this. And this is certainly something you should have. It's just another reason to communicate. You tell the customer that the quote is expiring and the file is closing—and not that you are expiring the quote or closing the file. They're just doing it on their own.

And if a customer comes back to you after expiration, you can always make an "exception." In fact, you can make as many "exceptions" as you'd like.

"But I don't want to bother my customers with these follow-ups. I sent them the quote. If they want it, they'll call me."

You are not bothering your customers when you follow up. You are not stepping on their toes. You are not taking their time.

You are showing them that you care. You are showing them that you are interested. You are telling them that they matter to you, and, unlike the competition, you are thinking about them and trying to help them.

You know what you will hear most when you follow up? "I'm glad you called," your customers will say.

"Thank you for reminding me," they will say. And then they will send you their money.

Your reward for being present, persistent, and interested will be more sales. Everybody wins.

5-Minute Selling Success

"I followed up on 12 quotes this week, and I closed half of them. Total closed amount surpasses $470,000. Among the six I didn't get: three gave me a reason, and the other three didn't get back to me. Oh well, their loss!" —Steve M., field sales engineer, manufacturer.

CHAPTER
30

ASK AND RECEIVE: HOW TO ALWAYS ASK FOR THE BUSINESS

When we ask for the business systematically, we are showing our customers that we are interested in helping them, and we are also systematically doing our customers a terrific favor. We are allowing our customers not to have to think about these products—which they get to buy from us *now*—again in the future.

Every salesperson knows that asking for the business consistently is extremely helpful to sales success. But few of us do it regularly and consistently.

The reason is always the same: Our fear. We don't want to turn off the customer.

"I don't want to offend-upset-anger-lose them. I've worked so hard to get this customer—what if I ask for the business, and they leave me altogether?"

They've been with you for 5 or 10 or 20 years. Do you think they'll leave you if you ask them when they'd like the order delivered? (That's one example of a pivot to the sale; see a bit later in this chapter for the complete list.)

Do you think they'll go to another supplier if you ask them when you can expect the purchase order? Of course not.

Remember, you serve these people incredibly well, and *you're not bothering them when you ask to help them.*

Plus, they trust you. They value your opinion. They *want* your help.

But we don't operate this way, do we? We operate as though we are an annoyance. A bother. A pain.

We are the opposite of those things. The sooner we can understand this and start to behave accordingly, the sooner our sales will quickly and significantly grow.

When we ask for the business systematically, we are also systematically doing our customers a terrific favor.

We are asking to help them, aren't we? We are asking to get them what they need, while also saving them time, right?

How do we save them time by asking for the business? They get to move on from this buying situation in a single, productive phone call. *And they don't have to think about it again.*

This is incredibly valuable to customers.

They're really busy, right? So if you can help them on a single call in a few minutes rather than multiple calls over days and weeks, they'll be grateful to you.

HERE ARE JUST SOME OF THE WAYS YOU CAN ASK FOR THE BUSINESS

Remember, these come from a mindset of helping the customer *now*, instead of later or not at all. They come from a position of belief in your great value and the strong relationships you build your business on.

*Even if you don't have a strong relationship with **this** customer, these questions will help you establish one!*

- Are you ready to buy?

- How many do you need? (Three is better than one! You won't have to worry about it again for a while.)

- How would you like to pay?

- Your credit or ours?

- Should we write it up?

- Your credit or mine?

- I'm ready to take the order now. (A pivot to the sale need not always be a question. Statements are fair game.)

- Ready to order?

- When would you like us to deliver it?

- What would you like me to add to this order? (A rDYK close!)

- Should we fill out the truck?

- I can have it to you Tuesday or Thursday. Which works better for you?

- We have 12 in the warehouse now, and I know this is an important item for you. Should I get them over to you?

- The price goes up next week, so I wanted to reach out to you. (*A terrifically effective closing question! This one has made my clients millions!*)

- Do you want to lock in the current pricing before it goes up?

As always, after you make any of these pivots to the sale, *be silent!*

Do not speak while the customer thinks. Why would you interrupt them?

You'd interrupt them because you're nervous. So be nervous quietly, okay? Be nervous and get the business. Success makes nervousness invisible.

HOW TO PIVOT TO THE NEXT COMMITMENT

Sometimes the customer isn't ready to buy at this moment, and you need another conversation. Or a meeting. Or a next event.

And because we should never hang up the phone or leave a meeting without the next commitment, here are your pivots to the next commitment:

- When should we talk again?

- What are our next steps?

- What do you want me to do next?

- When do you want me to follow up?

- When are we connecting next?

- I can call you on Wednesday or Friday. Which do you like?
- How much time do you need?
- I'd like to do this work with you, so when can we wrap this up?
- It's important to me to help you. When do you want me to reach out again?

A pivot to the sale is an expression of your interest in helping the customer.

Do not shy away from this. It's what you're good at.

Always remember, the customer wants to be helped by you. This is you asking to do it.

5-MINUTE SELLING SUCCESS

"I was having a conversation with a customer this week about a product they were considering trying, and I pivoted to the sales, asking if they would like one of the two units I have in stock. They thought for a moment and said, 'Sure, let's do it.' This is a new $85,000 in sales to us." —Katie S., counter sales, distributor.

31

CHAPTER

ASK YOUR CUSTOMERS WHAT PERCENT OF THEIR BUSINESS YOU HAVE

Tell your customers that you would like to help them more, and they will never say to you, "No, I don't want you to make my life easier today."

We salespeople are confident people. We have to be; there's no choice, really. Meekness and sales success do not go together, do they?

And it is because of this confidence that we so frequently overestimate the amount of business we are doing with our customers. Almost always, in my experience, salespeople *think* that we are doing more business with our customers than we actually are.

Ask salespeople what percent of a certain customer's business we have, and our answer will be higher than the real number. This is because we are in the muck with this customer on a regular basis.

We sell to them. We quote them, or propose. We service their account. We solve their problems. They take our time and mind space.

That's why it's shocking for most of us to think that we aren't taking care of *most* if not *all* of a customer's needs in our niche.

Almost always, the customer's *actual* percentage of business they're doing with you will surprise you. You *will* have more room to grow than you think—which is why we must ask our customers what percent of their business we have.

"Why would they tell me how much business I have of theirs?"

Because they consider you their partner and their friend. Because you save them time and save them money.

Because they trust you and value you. Because they *want* more of your help.

They don't want to buy from others. Help them buy more from you.

HERE IS YOUR LANGUAGE FOR THE PERCENT-OF-BUSINESS QUESTION

"Joe, what percent of your total business (in our category) do we have?"

At this point, Joe will be quiet, because he needs to think of the answer. *You* have been thinking about asking your question. *He* has been thinking about his stuff, not your stuff. So let him think!

Eventually, Joe will figure out the answer and give you a number: "About 50%, I'd guess."

You: "Interesting. What would it take to get 75% of your business? You're one of my best customers, and I'd like to help you more."

This will bring you into a discussion about what else they buy, and who they buy it from. Say to him: "Why don't you let *me* help you with that? I want to sell you that."

This is a pivot to the sale, covered in Chapter 30. The odds are very high that this exchange will reward you with more business—which is the point.

More help for your customer. And more money to take home for your family.

5-MINUTE
SELLING SUCCESS

"I was meeting with my customer and asked a percent-of-business question. I was very surprised to learn that they only give us half of their business. I honestly thought we had almost all of it. That's a lot of additional opportunity for us, and we've already started talking about several products that he hasn't been buying from us." —Tom G., outside sales, distributor.

CHAPTER 32

ASK FOR REFERRALS

People love giving referrals, because they love being helpful. But we don't ask for them much, so we don't get nearly as many referrals as we should and as we deserve.

$$W$$ hen my client companies launch their revenue growth programs, we track the quantity and outcome of each communication made by all customer-facing staff. Nearly all of the actions in this book are included in the counts.

Consistently, across all of my clients, the least-utilized technique (at first) is the one that this chapter covers: asking for referrals.

And this is under my careful guidance, where we work on optimizing sales mindsets and maximizing confidence, optimism, and boldness. We take proven steps to increase positivity and dramatically reduce fear.

In these projects, my salespeople clients start calling customers and prospects by the hundreds and, over time, as a company, by the thousands. They ask countless DYK questions and rDYK questions. They follow up on quotes and pivot to the sale.

But at the start of this work, only a few of them ask for referrals. They get them. And then they develop new customers from these referrals. And then these customers buy again, becoming extremely valuable repeat customers.

With time, as we discuss these successes, more people start to ask for referrals. Eventually, we get the sales teams to a critical mass of salespeople asking for referrals.

What keeps people from asking? I'll respond to the most frequent personal discomfort with referrals next.

"What if they don't like me enough to give me a referral? What if they don't want to? What if they get mad at me for asking?"

Most people are uncomfortable asking for referrals, even though customers love to give them. This is a terrible dichotomy: damaging to us, and harmful to customers.

Why is it harmful to customers? Because when you don't ask them for referrals, you are taking away from them the ability to help their friends and colleagues by connecting them to you.

They *want to* send their friends and colleagues to you—because they want to help them. If they have somebody who needs what you do, why wouldn't they want to send them to you?

Let me ask you a question. If a customer sends you a referral to somebody they know well, and that person buys from you, and you're happy, and the person who got referred is happy . . . who comes out looking best in that scenario?

That's right, the referrer does.

People love to give referrals. All we have to do is ask.

All those questions I listed? They're our "discomfort noise." They're our "fear noise."

When our discomfort and fear win, we hurt our customer, who doesn't get to help a friend or colleague. And we hurt the person who would have been (but won't be) referred to us, because they don't get to benefit from our help.

And we hurt our company because it doesn't get to onboard a new customer. And we hurt ourselves because we don't get to take home more money. And, of course, we hurt our family, who deserves the added income because they put up with us and support us.

All this to say . . . ask for the referral!

WHY WOULD THEY WANT TO REFER ME TO A COMPETITOR?

Unlike the concerns in the previous section, this one is *not* noise. It's real.

A customer would *not* want to refer you to a competitor. Which means, if you think this is something your customers might be thinking about, we need to ask for a referral to somebody who is *not* a competitor. You preemptively address this in your referral request, like in the first bullet point in the next section.

AFTER YOU ASK, DON'T SAY A WORD

After you ask one of those questions, do not speak. As discussed earlier in the book, do not nervously chatter your way out of a referral.

The customer will be quiet, but not because she is uncomfortable. She is quiet because she is thinking of somebody to refer to you. Do not interrupt this potentially lucrative (for you) thinking.

Look down. Pace if you need to. Count to 100 in your head if you must.

But don't you speak! There's a referral about to be named!

HERE IS YOUR LANGUAGE TO ASK FOR REFERRALS

There are two kinds of referrals we can ask for: an external one, to somebody at another company; and an internal one, to somebody who works at the same company as the customer you are asking.

Language to use for an external referral:

- "Who do you know, like yourself, who is not a competitor—perhaps they are in a different line of work than you—who would benefit from working with me the way you do?"

- "What customers or suppliers do you work with who can benefit from working with me the way you do?"

- "Who do you know in your executive (or networking) group who would benefit from working with me?"

Language to use for an internal referral:

- "Who else does what you do here? I'd like to help them, too."

- "Who do you work with in your department who buys what you buy? I'd love to help them like I help you."

- "Who can you connect me to in your Michigan (or any other) location?"

- "What counterparts do you have in other divisions of your company? I'd enjoy helping them, too."

Notes on language to use to ask for a referral:

- I'm sure you noticed that *every* referral request starts with *who*, not *do you know*. This is because I want my customers thinking about a name to give me, not a yes or no answer.

- Further, every question involves some form of *helping* the person who might be referred. I am helping my customers think about the value they can bring to their friend or colleague if they connect us.

WHAT TO DO IF THE CUSTOMER SAYS THEY'LL GET BACK TO YOU

In response to one of your referral questions, many of your customers might say some of version of "Let me think about it and get back to you."

This is a fair response. You asked them about something they have not been thinking about, and they are asking for some time.

But everybody knows the likelihood of this customer actually getting back to you with a referral is basically zero. Not because they don't want to give you a referral, but because they're extremely busy, and probably overwhelmed, and will likely not remember to think about your referral the moment your current referral conversation ends.

Do not accept this answer on its first iteration! ***Rather, help your customer think of somebody to refer to you.***

"I work with companies like yours—between \$X and \$Y in sales, and somebody in a similar position to yourself or even department A or B. Who do you know like this?"

And, again, wait quietly for the customer to think of somebody and answer your question. Remember: they *want to* help you.

In about half of these cases, you will be rewarded for your perseverance and helpfulness with a referral!

You're Not Done Yet: Two Last Questions to Ask

Now that you have a name—a *who*—you need a *how* and a *when*. This way, you'll know exactly what to do going forward.

"**Question #2:** Would you like to connect us, or would you prefer that I reach out to them and use your name?"

Almost always, the customer will offer to connect you—because people *like* to give referrals. They *want to* give you a referral. And frankly, they want the credit for this referral. This is why most people will want to send an email or make a call to tell their friend or colleague all about you.

Once you have a *how*, move on to your *when:*

"**Question #3:** So that I don't bother you, when do you think you might get to it?"

The customer will name a date. This is when you follow up.

Summarize the referral, reviewing the name, the pathway, and the date, and make one last confirmation: "If I don't hear from you by this date, is it okay to follow up with you?"

The customer will, of course, agree, and you're in business.

This is how to ask for a referral. You need all three things: the *who*, the *how*, and the *when*.

And, most importantly, just ask. Customers will be happy to send you to their people. Because you're going to make them look good!

5-MINUTE
SELLING SUCCESS

"I was on the phone with a good customer, and I went through a series of our communications. First I asked a DYK about one product, and then about another product. This resulted in a new quote being sent. Then I asked a reverse DYK, and the customer told me about a product they buy elsewhere that they'd like me to quote. Then I asked who their contact person is in their Minneapolis branch, and they gave me a name and number! I said, 'Thank you very much, what about in Wisconsin? Who should I talk to there?' It's a new branch they just bought, so there's no contact in Wisconsin yet. It was a great five-minute call that resulted in a new quote, a new pre-quote opportunity, and a referral to a new prospective customer. Time well spent!" —Jon J., outside sales, manufacturer.

CHAPTER 33

SEND HANDWRITTEN NOTES

Handwritten notes make us memorable for months and years.

Emails make us forgotten instantly.

T hink back. Can you remember the last handwritten note you received?

Most people can, because it's so rare to get one.

Can you picture it? Who was it from? You can remember the person's name, right?

Do you remember the size of the paper it was written on? Full sheet or smaller? Or maybe a card that folded? Regardless, you can picture it. Most people can.

Remember what it said? When I ask this in my speeches and workshops, most audience members can remember *exactly* what the note was about, with many reciting it back to me word for word.

What color was the ink? Blue or black, or something funkier? Finally, was the writing in cursive or print letters?

Chances are, whether your last handwritten note came last week our three months ago, you can recall all those details. Right?

Next: Think back to that day . . . and list all the emails you got.

Who were they from? What were they about? What did people want from you? What was pitched at you, marketed to you, promoted to you, *shouted* at you?

Can you make a complete list? Of course not. In fact, most people cannot even name a single email they got with certainty on a particular day weeks or months ago.

And that is the power of handwritten notes. We remember them actively, while we actively put emails out of our minds.

Handwritten notes are memorable and caring. *Handwritten notes honor us as recipients.* Handwritten notes show us that we matter to the senders.

They stopped what they were doing and thought about us for several minutes, *which is no small thing.*

And from a sales perspective, sending handwritten notes makes magic.

Email makes our customers forget us, while handwritten notes make them remember us. Email is annoying, while handwritten notes are thoughtful.

Email is trashed; handwritten notes are treasured. I've kept some notes for years. So, probably, have you.

Handwritten notes show our customers that we care about them.

We will probably be the only ones who send our customers a handwritten note on this day. And this week. And this month. And, probably, this quarter.

We will stand out from the crowd of competitors who don't—who don't care enough to do this. Our customers will remember.

SEND HUMAN NOTES, NOT THANK YOU NOTES

If people do get a handwritten note when it's not Christmas or their birthday, it is usually some form of thank you note. *Thank you for your time. Thank you for meeting with me. Thank you for your business.*

I like to send human notes rather than thank you notes.

Think back to your last conversation with the person you are sending your note to. What did you talk about? What came up?

Did you talk about a vacation they took? Or a hobby? Their new car? Their kids? Their home? Write a line or two about that.

For example:

"It was so nice to learn about your kids and the amazing work they are doing in college. I bet you're really proud of them. Heck, *I* am proud of them!"

Or:

"How's that hot new ride doing for you? It's probably awesome to drive, and I can't wait to check it out the next time we're together."

See how that's so much better than simply writing "Thank you"? Write human notes, not thank you notes.

"But do these notes really matter any more? Nobody sends them, do they?"

Exactly. Nobody sends them—which is why you should.

To stand out from the competition. To be better than the competition. Because *you are better than the competition.* This is a way of communicating it.

It's a way of showing your customers that you are thinking about them. They will appreciate this greatly. They will be grateful for it.

And in short order, they will reward you with more business for it.

5-MINUTE SELLING SUCCESS

"I've written quite a few handwritten notes since the training with you. So far, three customers who got a note have called me after receiving it to thank me. Of course, I asked if they needed anything while we are on the phone, and wouldn't you know it, they *all* made a purchase right there on the phone. It was several thousand dollars altogether." —Marie M., customer service, manufacturer.

CHAPTER 34

SEND WEEKLY HIGH-VALUE EMAIL COMMUNI-CATIONS

These aren't sales emails. You're not pitching or leading with discounts like most junk emails.

You're helping your customers and prospects with real value. They will be grateful for this.

Some of the most suc-
cessful salespeople I've ever worked with send their customers and prospect list a weekly email. Very few do this, and the
ones who do, almost as a rule, outperform everyone else.

This mailing is independent of anything the company
sends. It comes from *you.* Which means that *you* will be emailing your customers, *and* your company should as well.

It's a high-value, regular email that arrives on the same
day each week. In general, these mailings are very short and
can be read in their entirety in about one minute.

HERE IS WHAT YOUR EMAIL
CAN INCLUDE

A successful weekly mailing can contain any one or two of the
items listed next. I repeat: these are brief mailings. Pick one
or two of these things and email them weekly, and you will

be helping your customers and prospects far more than the competition:

- A quick summary of an industry article you found on an editorial web site that would provide value to your list. This article can be about:
  - Industry news
  - Tips, tricks, and advice
  - Economic forecasts and predictions
  - Anything else that your customers and prospects would find useful
- A list of currently stocked products and what's incoming this week.
- If you are in a commodity business, you can simply provide the latest commodity price!
- A DYK question. Simply feature a product or service that you can provide your customers and prospects. Use the email to educate them on how you can help them. You might consider including a DYK question in every one of these emails, in a quick line or two. Just name the product, and add a sentence about what it is or does. Some of my distributor clients simply list lines that they carry from their suppliers here, as a reminder to customers. Service clients list one offering at a time.
- A (very) quick personal update, if you wish. In no more than one brief paragraph, share your latest news—focus on business or personal.
- Every email should have your contact information and direct phone number.

Make these fun for you.

You know these people. They know you. You have relationships with them. They will appreciate hearing from you.

"But people get so much spam now, I'm just going to be another junk email they're going to delete."

You've been reading long enough now: whose discomfort is this?

These aren't selling messages. You're not pitching or leading with discounts like most junk emails.

You're helping your customers and prospects with real value. They will be grateful for this. Some of my salespeople clients have had customers pick up the phone and call them to thank them for these emails.

You will find inquiries coming in regularly in reply to these emails.

Will some people unsubscribe? Sure, but they're entitled to. They're adults.

And just because they unsubscribe from this mailing doesn't mean you have to stop communicating with them altogether. You can still call them. You can still email them one-on-one.

Don't worry about offending people. Some people will be offended no matter how carefully you tiptoe, so what's the point?

Worry about helping more people more with your amazing value. That's the secret sauce to selling more.

5-Minute
Selling Success

"I started sending my customers a weekly email, in addition to the one we send as a company. My email simply included the price of our commodity, which updates daily, and a quick thought or two about the direction of the market. I sent this to *my* customers and prospects only. A few things started to happen: first, they regularly write me thanking me for the information and telling me that nobody else sends them anything like it. Second, my customers started replying to these emails, with requests for pricing, and orders.

I think the emails remind them to place their orders.

I spend 10 minutes writing the email, if that.

And I've sold hundreds of thousands of dollars in product as a result." —Brian H., outside sales, commodity distributor.

PART FIVE

LAUNCH!

CHAPTER

35

What a Typical 5-Minute Selling Week Looks Like

Here is your implementation
recipe for success:
1. Quickly plan.
2. Quickly do.
3. Track your results.

First, on Sunday or very early on Monday, take three minutes to fill out your Proactive Call Planner.

5' MINUTE SELLING   PROACTIVE CALL PLANNER

My Best Customers Who Can Buy More	Customers Who Used to Buy but Stopped

My Smaller and Medium Customers Who Can Buy More from Me	Customers Who Recently Received Products or Services — Follow Up

Customers I Haven't Talked to in Three Months or More	PROSPECTS I Am Having Active Buying Conversations With — Follow Up

PROSPECTS I Once Talked to, but They Did Not Buy — Follow Up	PROSPECTS I Know Are Buying Elsewhere

Write names in any category here. It doesn't matter where you write them.

Reference your emails, text messages, notebooks, order histories, and anything else you have that can help you think of people's names.

Spend three minutes on this at the most.

Next, take another three minutes (maximum) and fill out this Weekly Follow-Up Planner:

WEEKLY
FOLLOW-UP PLANNER

Week of (Date):

Customers with Pre-Quote or Pre-Proposal Opportunities to Follow Up With	Customers With Quotes or Proposals to Follow Up With	Current Customers Who Can Buy More Who I Can Follow Up With (And What to Offer Them)

Again, write names in all three columns. The first column is for pre-quote opportunities, the second column is for quotes to follow up on, and the third column is for customers who can buy more.

Don't just work from your head. Go into reference material that will remind you of people who you are not thinking about.

Now, keep these two planners with you throughout the week. They should be in front of your eyes—which means they should be on top of your desk or on your bulletin board. Or with you in your car, if you drive to sales calls (not on the windshield, though). Or on your clipboard, if you work in a showroom with customers.

I want you to see these documents multiple times per day: as much to remind you to *make* the follow-up calls as to remind you *who* to call.

Their main purpose is to remind you to *make* the communications. Their secondary purpose is instruct you *who* to communicate with.

NOW, GO TO WORK

First thing in the morning, it would be great if you found time to make one or two proactive calls to somebody on your Proactive Call Planner.

You will probably leave a voicemail (Chapter 15), so that's a 30-second effort. If you catch somebody live, you'll have a pleasant, positive conversation to start your day. You'll feel good about it.

Write down what you do (even the voicemails you leave) on your 5-Minute Action Tracker.

Then, turn to the work of the day—the incoming onslaught from customers with problems and urgencies. Resolve their problems. And then, if they are happy, ask a DYK. Or a few of them.

Then ask an rDYK. Then pivot to the sale.

Record your actions on the 5-Minute Selling Action Tracker:

ACTION TRACKER

Week of (Date):

Day / Date	Customer / Prospect Name	Proactive Action Code	What You Said	What They Said	$$ E, EA, Q/P, C

Total Opened Business: **Total Opened Annualized:**   **Total Quoted / Proposed:**   **Total Closed:**

Spend no more than 20 seconds writing down your actions.

If a single conversation features multiple efforts (for example, you asked three DYKs and one rDYK, and you pivoted to the sale), record *all of them* on a single line. You'd write "3DYK, rDYK, Pivot" in the Proactive Action Code column.

Record what you said and what the customer said. And estimate the value of the interaction.

If you've opened up a new opportunity, estimate the current sale and also its annual value: write "E$200" (the estimated value of *this* upcoming order is $200), and "EA$10,000" if you expect them to order it once a week, or 50 times in a year.

If you have a free moment in between incoming calls, send a quick quote follow-up. Email is okay here (cringe). You may choose to take a couple of minutes and send a handful of quote follow-up emails all at once.

Record these follow-ups, and any quotes you may send throughout the day on your Quote Tracker:

QUOTE TRACKER

Week of (Date):

Quote Date	Quote #	Customer / Prospect Name	Products / Services	Amount $	Follow-Up 1		Follow-Up 2		Follow-Up 3	
					How	When	How	When	How	When

Each day, make your one or two proactive calls first thing. Then, throughout the day, ask your DYKs, rDYKs, and pivots. Record things quickly in your Action Tracker.

At the end of the week, add up the total dollars in all four categories (estimated for *this* order, estimated annually, quoted, and sold), and write them down at the bottom.

Save your trackers. Have a pile of them in chronological order, kept together with a binder clip. Or use a three-hole-punch and put them into a binder.

Keep them because:

1. They are a powerful record of success.

2. They are full of opportunities to follow up on.

Review them briefly at the start of each week, or at the end. Give them a few minutes weekly. They're a gold mine of success and opportunity.

This is how to work the 5-Minute Selling System. Quickly plan and quickly do. Keep a brief record of your proactive actions. And enjoy the tsunami of new sales you're about to open up.

CHAPTER

36

5-Minute Selling Scripts and Language

Start with my language if you'd like,
but the sooner this becomes
your language, the sooner
you will sell more.

As soon as you can, use your own
words that are comfortable for you.

Here is all the language from all of the actions in one place. Use this to quickly reference what to say.

One quick point: the sooner this goes from being my language to *your* language, the better you will do with it.

I'm giving you language in this book to get you started. If you can, use your own words that are comfortable for you. If you don't know what your own words may be yet, start with mine, and move to yours as soon as possible.

The success from these efforts kicks into overdrive when they are implemented using your language rather than mine.

FOR CALLING YOUR BEST CUSTOMERS

"Joe, it's Chris. How are you? How's everything going this week? Listen, I was thinking that it has been a long time since I've called you without an urgent matter to discuss. You good? How's your family? Do you need anything from us on what we're currently doing? I'm glad things are going well there."

Now pivot to a rDYK question: "Listen, I know you have other suppliers, because you've talked about them before. What else do you buy elsewhere that we can help you with? I'd love to handle those headaches for you, our way."

Or ask some DYK questions: "I know you've been buying these products from us for a long time, but I wanted to let you know we also have products x and y and z that you probably need. Why don't you buy those from us? I'd like to help you with those."

FOR CALLING YOUR *FORMER* BEST CUSTOMERS

"Hi Joe, it's Chris(tine) calling. How are you?! It's been a long time since we've talked. What's the latest in your world? How is your family? Kids good?"

Now, gently pivot to the reason for the call: "Great. You know, I was just thinking that there was a time when you were one of my very best customers. I miss those times! (Laugh.) I'd like to have you back in that position, at the top of my list."

Check their order history: "Are you still buying a lot of product x or y? Because we still sell that, and I'd love to be able to help you with that again."

Ask a rDYK question: "What are you buying elsewhere these days? Give me a chance at that business. I won't let you down. It'll be my top priority to make you happy."

FOR CALLING SMALL AND MID-SIZED CUSTOMERS

Be open and transparent: "It has been a long time since we've talked, and it's important to me to connect with you. How have you been? How is your family?"

Now pivot to a rDYK question: "I was thinking about you and wondering, what are you working on these days that I may be able to help you with?"

For Calling Customers You Haven't Talked to in Three Months or More

"Mary, it's Joe. How are you? Listen, I know it has been a long time since we've talked, but I was thinking about you, and I wanted to pick up the phone. What's happening? How's your work going?"

Pivot to how their buying experience with your company is going: "Mary, how are we doing for you? Are we treating you well? It's important to me that you're happy."

Ask your rDYK: "What other products or services can I help with, Mary? What else do you need?"

Now, ask for the business (pivot to the sale): "I'd like to sell that to you. Do you want me to add that to your next order?"

For Calling Customers Who Used to Buy but Stopped

"Joe, it's Mike. How are you? It has been a while since we talked. I was thinking about you and wondering how you are doing. Is everything going well? How's your family?"

Pivot to the business portion of the discussion: "How's it going without us?" (Laugh.)

"What can I help with? I'd sure enjoy the opportunity to work together again."

For Calling Customers Who Just Received an Order

"Hi Ellen, it's Joe. I hope you're doing well. Hey, I wanted to call and see if that last order arrived okay. Everything go well with that? Do you need anything else from me on this?"

If the customer brings up any issues or questions, address them. Otherwise, if they're happy, move on to one of the fast communications:

Ask a DYK: "I'm so glad things went well, Ellen. Did you know we can also help you with product x and product y just as well as we did here with this one?"

Or ask a rDYK: "I'm glad you're happy, Ellen. Now, what other products or services would you like me to take care of for you?"

Or ask for a referral: "That's great to hear, Ellen. Listen, I was just wondering, who do you know like yourself who would also benefit from working with me the way that you have?"

FOR CALLING PROSPECTS YOU ARE IN ACTIVE BUYING CONVERSATIONS WITH

"Tom, I was thinking about you and wanted to follow up on our last conversation. Helping you is important to me. Where are you at on this? I'd love to start working with you on this."

FOR CALLING PROSPECTS WHO YOU KNOW ARE CURRENTLY BUYING FROM THE COMPETITION

"Tom, I know you're with X Competitor currently, and I wanted to reach out to you. I actually have a customer similar to you. His name is [insert name — of course, not a competitor], and he says that working with us is twice as fast as the competition and that he can reach us any time including weekends and evenings. Now I'd like to help you this way. Would you give me an opportunity to help you this way? What are you working on these days that I can help you with?"

For Calling Prospects You Once Talked to, but Who Never Bought

"Tom, I hope you are well. It has been a while since we've talked, and I was thinking about you. Where are you at on that order (or work) we talked about? I'd sure love to help you with that."

To Ask the DYK Question and Expand the Products and Services You Sell to Your Customers

- "Did you know we can also help you with product x?"
- "Do you also need product y?"
- "What about product z?"
- "How are you on product a?"
- "Do you need product b with that?"
- "Should I also add product c?"

To Ask the Reverse DYK Question and Learn What Else Your Customer Buys Elsewhere

- "What else are you buying elsewhere that *I* can help you with?"
- "What else do you need that we can provide?"

- "What do you buy from those other suppliers that you always complain about? Let *me* help you with that!"
- "What else do you need quoted or proposed?"
- "What other projects do you have coming up?"
- "What are you having trouble getting quoted?"
- "What's next?"
- "What products or services are you having trouble getting quoted?"
- "What's on your wish list?"

To Expand Your Percentage of Business with a Customer

"Joe, what percent of your total business (in our category) do we have?"

Customer: "About 50%, I'd guess."

You: "Interesting. What would it take get 75% of your business? You're one of my best customers, and I'd like to help you more."

To Sell Based on a Customer's Order History

- "I was looking back at your order history and noticed you used to buy product x or y. Do you need more of that?"
- "I see that it has been six months since you've ordered product x. How are you doing with that?"
- "Hey Joe, you haven't bought this in some time. Let me send some out so we can make sure you don't run out."

TO FOLLOW UP ON QUOTES (QFU)

Three emails that close 20% of outstanding quotes:

1. "Did you get the quote I sent you? These things tend to get picked off by spam filters. Please confirm it got to you."

2. "I was just thinking about you. Where are you at on that quote we discussed?"

3. "Haven't heard from you. A gentle reminder that our quote is going to expire. Please let me know within 24 hours if you want to move forward. If not, thank you for the opportunity, and I hope we can come together on something soon."

TO ASK FOR THE BUSINESS (PIVOT)

- "Are you ready to buy?"
- "How many do you need? (Three is better than one! You won't have to worry about it again for a while.)"
- "How would you like to pay?"
- "Your credit or ours?"
- "Should we write it up?"
- "Your credit or mine?"
- "I'm ready to take the order now."

TO ASK FOR A REFERRAL (REFER)

1. "Who do you know like yourself [at another division or another firm—pick one!] who I can help like I help you?"

2. "Would you like me to reach out and use your name, or would you like to connect us?"

3. "So that I don't bother you, when do you think you might get to that?"

TO SEND A HANDWRITTEN NOTE

Think back to your last conversation with the person you are sending your note to: What did you talk about? What came up? Did you talk about a vacation they took? Or a hobby? Their new car? Their kids? Their home? Write a line or two about that:

"It was so nice to learn about your kids and the amazing work they are doing in college. I bet you're really proud of them. Heck, *I* am proud of them!"

CHAPTER 37

THE WORK
IS THE
MAGIC
BULLET

I get to work with exceptional companies.

Most of my clients have been operating for *generations*. They're in mature industries, filled with "experienced" salespeople, and when they get to me, their sales have often been flat or decreasing. For years.

All of them add significant additional sales from this work. Some add 10% annually. Others add 20%. Still others add 30%—and these firms are often in the hundreds of millions of dollars in annual sales and growing like this. It's all tracked and attributed to the actions laid out in this book.

As I've told you throughout this book, individual salespeople's sales frequently double and triple by doing this work. And I keep repeating this on purpose, because I'm hoping you see it enough times that you feel *your own personal sales can grow like this, too.*

People ask me, what's the secret to this kind of growth? What's the magic bullet?

My answer: *the work is the secret.*

There is no magic bullet. There is not *one thing* that you can buy or do one time to grow your sales like this. There is only the work.

There is only the communication with customers and prospects.

The secret is the consistent, systematic implementation of confident, optimistic, proactive communications to customers and prospects.

That's what grows the sales. There's your secret. The work is the secret.

You now have everything you need.

You have the planners and the trackers and the mindsets and the actions and the language scripts. I've even preemptively overcome your objections in each of the chapters on proactive communications.

You now have everything you need to bring home more money to your family. And to help your customers more. And to rescue prospects from the competition.

You know exactly what to do.

You know what the secret is. The secret is the work. And you know exactly what this means.

Will you do it?

Will you do the work?

CHAPTER

38

5-Minute Selling Mindset Manifesto

Here's a quick piece of self-talk for you to quickly say to yourself as you prepare for your next phone call or in-person meeting. Use it as a mantra to motivate these proactive actions as well.

I bring my customers and prospects great value and care.

They are with me because they trust me.

They consider me a friend and a family member.

I care for them, and they care for me.

I will help them more.

They want this from me.

I will offer additional products and services.

I will follow up.

I will ask for the business.

They deserve this from me.

If I don't do these things, I am hurting them.

Other suppliers don't do what they say.

I am better than them.

Other suppliers wait for the customer to find the problem, but I fix the problem before the customer even knows about it.

Other suppliers let my customers down.

I will rescue my valued customers from this terrible experience with the competition.

I owe this to them and to my family.

I want to help my customers more.

My customers pay more to buy from me than from others, and they know this.

They pay more to work with me because they know I won't let them down.

They know I will always be there for them.

My customers just want me to be present.

They just want to know that I care.

I will be present.

I will show them that I care.

And because of all this, my sales will grow.

Which is what I deserve.

INDEX